Cities
without
Suburbs

Cities without Suburbs

Third Edition: A Census 2000 Update

David Rusk

 Published by Woodrow Wilson Center Press, Washington, D.C.

Distributed by The Johns Hopkins University Press, Baltimore and London

EDITORIAL OFFICES
Woodrow Wilson Center Press
One Woodrow Wilson Plaza
1300 Pennsylvania Avenue, NW
Washington, D.C. 20004-3027
Telephone 202-691-4010
http://www.wilsoncenter.org

Order from
The Johns Hopkins University Press
Hamden Station
P.O. Box 50370
Baltimore, Md. 21211
Telephone 1-800-537-5487
http://www.jhupbooks.com

Library of Congress Cataloging-in-Publication Data

Rusk, David.
    Cities without suburbs : a Census 2000 update / David Rusk.—3rd ed.
        p.   cm — (Woodrow Wilson Center special studies)
    Includes bibliographical references and index.
    ISBN 1-930365-13-6 (cloth : alk. paper) — ISBN 1-930365-14-4 (pbk. :
alk. paper)
        1. Urban policy—United States.   2. Metropolitan government—United
States.   3. Metropolitan areas—United States.   I. Title.   II. Series.
HT123.R84   2003
307.76′0973—dc21

                                                                        2003006734

To Delcia,
my wife
and
partner

Contents

Boxes

Preface

This short book is written for public policymakers. Its intended audience is our new president and his administration, U.S. senators and representatives, state governors, legislators, city and county elected officials—and key staff everywhere who behind the scenes help make American government work. I also wrote the book for thoughtful and concerned citizens who are prepared to think in a different way about what has happened in and around their communities and who will spur their public officials to take decisive action.

This was the audience I targeted in the preface to the first edition of *Cities without Suburbs*. My book found another unexpected readership as well—thousands of college students for whom this short (and relatively inexpensive) book was adopted for coursework. Since its publication in April 1993, *Cities without Suburbs* has clearly had an impact on those audiences. Although hardly received on the scale of the latest best-selling novel, the original book went through seven printings, encouraging the publishers to issue a revised edition in 1995. Its themes were reviewed or discussed in several hundred magazine and newspaper articles and increasingly cited in scholarly works. *Cities without Suburbs* also helped launch a new phase of my career. During the past decade I have been invited to speak and consult in over 100 metropolitan areas, ranging in size from Sharon, Pennsylvania, to New York, New York, covering the country from Miami, Florida, to Seattle, Washington.

If all this sounds too self-congratulatory, I must acknowledge the tremendous difference between the world of opinion and the world of decision. Has *Cities without Suburbs* really changed anything anywhere? Are there any communities in this country where life is better as a result of my efforts?

The most hopeful answer is "just barely." Some cities, such as Fort Wayne, Memphis, and Springfield, Ohio, have been moved to reinvigorate their annexation policies. A handful of others

(Augusta, Louisville, and Kansas City, Kansas) have successfully consolidated with their counties. To discourage suburban sprawl and urban disinvestment, some states, such as Maryland and Tennessee, have adopted more stringent growth management laws. A short, but growing list of communities has enacted inclusionary zoning laws that mandate integrating modest proportions of low-income housing into new, larger, middle-class housing developments. The federal Department of Housing and Urban Development is tearing down high-density warehouses for the poor and replacing them with mixed-income urban villages. And in 1997, the Congress, in effect, repealed the capital gains tax on home sales—an action that should strengthen older community housing markets in the long run. For each of these examples, my contribution ranged from being only a marginal part of the background noise to making a significant contribution.

Why a new *Cities without Suburbs: Census 2000 Update?* A lesser reason is that this new book is enriched by a decade's experience in the field and by my greater familiarity with the growing body of scholarly work. But the larger reason is that Census 2000 now provides a penetrating new scan of urban America's demographic, social, and economic trends down to the neighborhood level.

A decade later, do the lessons I proposed about urban America still hold up? To highlight what may be different emerging trends, many of the book's tables will summarize results not just from 1950 to 2000, but also during the 1990s. However, to jump to the end of the story (and only slightly modifying the French), "the more things change, the more they remain (almost) the same."

The foundation of this book, first and foremost, is my practical experience—political and managerial—as mayor of Albuquerque from 1977 to 1981. Four years as chief executive of the largest city in New Mexico may not, in some readers' opinion, qualify me as an expert on America's cities. But Albuquerque is a bigger city—and its city hall runs a bigger city government—than such literally big league cities as Atlanta, Buffalo, Cincinnati, Miami, Minneapolis (and St. Paul), Oakland, Pittsburgh, and St. Louis. Within ten or twenty years at most, Albuquerque's population will surpass that of the cities of Baltimore, Cleveland, Milwaukee, New Orleans, and Washington, D.C.

All this because, as a central city, Albuquerque is growing, and the others are shrinking! The reason why an Albuquerque grows and a Baltimore, Cleveland, or St. Louis shrinks—what I call a city's elasticity—is essential for understanding the relative health of cities across the nation today.

Other practical career experiences shape this book. Before becoming mayor, I spent three years as a state legislator in New Mexico and five years as a civil rights and antipoverty worker with the Washington Urban League. Also valuable was my federal government experience as the U.S. Manpower Administration's legislative services chief.

Importantly, this book is the product of painstaking, hands-on research. My wife, Delcia, and I have passed endless days unearthing data from old census publications. My long backward look over the past five decades forced us laboriously to copy and then to enter over 500,000 pieces of information into the database of our personal computer. Beyond census data, for some communities, I have searched out property assessment reports, copied down key data from school-by-school report cards on the Internet, and analyzed realtors' and homebuilders' reports on home sales prices. With gratitude, I have eagerly seized upon other analysts' cataloging of urban phenomena from David Miller's Metropolitan Power Diffusion Index to Richard Florida's Creativity Index to Myron Orfield's visually provocative, five-color maps.

I originally decided to write *Cities without Suburbs* as an act of hope and faith. I believe that the problem this book addresses— the urban problem—is the toughest issue in American society. It goes right to the heart of the deep-rooted fears about race and social class that have had so much to do with shaping urban America today.

Yet a decade's active involvement in over 100 communities has both sharpened my understanding of this challenge and sustained my optimism. The issue is not so much urban poverty overall as highly concentrated urban poverty in certain central cities and older suburbs, in poverty-impacted neighborhoods, and among blacks and Hispanics (as contrasted with non-Hispanic whites). In America in 2000, there were 14.4 million poor whites compared to 8.0 million poor blacks and 7.7 million poor Hispanics. In a typical metropolitan area, however, where 78 percent of all poor people lived, three out of four poor whites lived in middle-class neighborhoods scattered widely across the whole region; by contrast, three out of four poor blacks and one out of two poor Hispanics lived in poverty-impacted, inner-city neighborhoods.

Inner-city poverty appears insurmountable because of this very high degree of concentration. Yet America is not some Third World country where the poor are many and the middle class are few. Of every 100 residents of America's metropolitan areas, about six are poor and white—and they are mostly integrated into middle-class society. Of every 100 residents, only about six are poor and black or Hispanic—but they are much more isolated from the middle-class mainstream. Middle-class America has the capacity to absorb poor blacks and Hispanics as it already absorbs most poor whites. What is lacking too often is not the resources but the political will to do so.

Nevertheless, seen in this regional context, the manageable scale of the problem is one source of my optimism. And I have met and worked with so many concerned and engaged citizens and organizations in the hundred communities that I have visited that I have confidence that the political will to change can be generated as well.

My colleague john powell has said that "if racism were to vanish overnight in America, little would change, because the economic incentives of the current system are so powerful for those who now benefit." What this decade has taught me most is that building political coalitions to achieve fundamental reforms in the rules of the game is hard, time-consuming work.

As Winston Churchill once commented, "at the end of the day, the American people will do the right thing—after they have exhausted all other alternatives." I have faith that our political debates, as Abraham Lincoln testified in his first inaugural address, will be "again touched, as surely they will be, by the angels of our better nature." The policy debate must be framed not as a choice between conservative and liberal philosophies, but as a choice between policies that work and policies that do not work. The purpose of *Cities without Suburbs: Census 2000 Update* is to point out what works.

Acknowledgments

I must begin by thanking all the thousands of public officials, urban professionals, citizen activists, college professors, and their students who have read the first two editions of *Cities without Suburbs.* Without your interest there would be no third edition: *Census 2000 Update,* and many have made comments and suggestions that have contributed to this being, I believe, a much better book than its predecessors.

I must also express my gratitude to the many committed community leaders I have met in the more than 250 organizations who have sponsored my visits to over 100 communities during the past decade. They have been my mentors in an ever-fascinating, postgraduate seminar on urban America. Their insights and experiences enrich this book.

In a more direct sense this book would not have been possible without the support of two extraordinary institutions. The first is the Woodrow Wilson International Center for Scholars, which invited me to serve as a guest scholar first in summer 1992 and again in summer 2002 in order to complete the research and writing of *Cities without Suburbs.* In particular, I received invaluable assistance from my research associates, Daniel Green (1992), now a successful attorney, and Ricky Moore (2002), a very gifted thinker, writer, and (more than most members of his generation) computer maven from whom I learned much. I am particularly grateful to Joseph Brinley, director of the Woodrow Wilson Center Press, and Carol Belkin Walker, editor, for their wise guidance and support.

The second institution is the United States Bureau of the Census. In my experience, the Census Bureau provides an understanding of our nation's demographic, social, and economic trends that is unmatched internationally. Moreover, with the support of its ever-helpful professional staff, it has been a pleasure through the years to be able to browse among the stacks of the Census Bureau library and pull off the shelf any census publication going back to 1790.

Throughout this decade my wife, Delcia, has been my business manager, data entry assistant, travel companion, best critic, both my rudder and my even keel. The professional life on which this book is based would have been impossible without her love and support.

Introduction: Framing the Issue

To discuss urban policy it is helpful to have a common view of the urban problem. Creating more jobs, building housing, constructing streets, highways, water and sewer systems, controlling pollution, and generating needed public revenues are common issues for urban areas everywhere, but collectively they do not seem to add up to America's urban problem. In fact, compared with many societies abroad, America does not really have an urban problem as such. Most urban Americans are better employed, better housed, better served by transportation systems and public facilities, and live in better environmental conditions than much of the rest of the world. America's real urban problem is racial and economic segregation that has created an underclass in many of America's major urban areas.

Segregating poor urban Blacks and Hispanics has spawned physically decaying, revenue-strapped, poverty-impacted, crime-ridden "inner cities." These inner cities are isolated from their "outer cities"—wealthier, growing, still largely white suburbs.

Debate over urban policy has focused typically on only a handful of America's largest inner cities. By contrast, this book will look at all urban areas and examine in detail 119 urban areas with populations of 250,000 or more. Also, my focus will be on entire metropolitan areas—cities and suburbs.

This broader perspective will yield, I hope, greater clarity about what has been happening in urban America. There are lessons to be learned from many urban areas that are rarely analyzed. There are bad lessons to be drawn from areas such as Harrisburg, Pennsylvania, and Syracuse, New York, and success stories to be learned, for example, from Madison, Wisconsin, and my own Albuquerque.

In highly segregated urban areas—no matter how wealthy area-wide—concentrated poverty, joblessness, and crime compound each other; as a result, their central cities are failing. In more integrated urban areas—even when poorer area-wide—

1

poverty, dependency, and crime lack a certain critical mass; their central cities are succeeding.

In about half of the country's large urban areas, social and economic inequities are severe. In the other half, however, good timing, good luck, and good public policy—which come to focus in what I call a city's elasticity—have combined to create more successful communities for whites, blacks, and Hispanics alike.

From my research on all 331 metropolitan areas in the United States, I have derived 26 lessons about what has been happening in urban America since World War II. The statistical analysis typically begins with the 1950 census and ends with the 2000 census. The first four lessons stated in chapter I are supported by data drawn from all 331 metropolitan areas within the country. Thereafter, in an effort to communicate in as clear and jargon-free manner as possible, I illustrate the remaining 22 lessons by contrasting 7 specific pairs of metropolitan areas: Houston and Detroit, Columbus and Cleveland, Nashville and Louisville, Indianapolis and Milwaukee, Albuquerque and Syracuse, Madison and Harrisburg, Raleigh and Richmond. These lessons, however, were originally framed by analyzing trends in 119 metro areas with more than 250,000 inhabitants.

In chapter II, I divide these 119 larger metro areas into 5 broad categories. For each of these broad categories, I then restate lessons introduced in chapter I.

In chapter III, I discuss strategies for stretching cities. Unlike the original edition of *Cities without Suburbs,* the *Census 2000 Update* will not focus as much on policies that lead formally to more unified local governance, such as municipal annexation powers and city-county consolidation. Altering local political boundaries is legally impossible throughout New England, New York, New Jersey, and Pennsylvania, and pragmatically impossible around many older central cities, particularly in much of the Midwest.

As a consequence, I will devote increased attention to what one critic called elasticity mimics—regional growth management policies, regional fair share housing policies (inclusionary zoning), and regional tax-base sharing policies. (These are discussed at great length in my *Inside Game/Outside Game.*) Adopting these recommendations (changing the "rules of the game") can profoundly improve the long-term outlook for central cities and their regions.

Finally, chapter IV restates my conclusions and offers some final observations.

This *Census 2000 Update* benefits from an invaluable, post-publication insight regarding the original *Cities without Suburbs*: what an author thinks he writes may not be what some readers read. So let me be clear about what are (and are not) the principal themes of *Cities without Suburbs: Census 2000 Update.*

1) The book is primarily an explanation why, in the Age of Sprawl, some cities, as municipalities, are relatively healthy and growing and others are relatively troubled and declining.

2) The book argues that "Big Box" regions (with their steadily expanding central cities and larger, sometimes countywide school districts) implicitly facilitate greater racial and economic integration while "little boxes" regions (where the core city and its school system are trapped within inflexible boundaries, surrounded by myriad independent suburbs and school districts) are characterized by greater racial and economic segregation.

3) This book does not (nor did it ever originally intend to) propose a theory of economic development, although I certainly contend that both cities and suburbs are integral components of regional economies.

I often told Albuquerque audiences that New Mexico is one of the few places where a Puccini, a Pulaski, and a Goldstein could all be called "Anglo." Throughout the book, when I refer to "white," I mean "Anglo"—that is, non-Hispanic whites. I do not mean to slight either the problems or achievements of urban Asians and Native Americans by not focusing on them. From my analysis, however, it is only around whites, blacks, and Hispanics that social and political attitudes in America revolve with sufficient force and magnitude to shape patterns of urban growth.

Chapter I

Lessons from Urban America

Despite the romance of the frontier, the true land of opportunity in America for over 150 years has been the cities. From farms and foreign lands, urban immigrants flocked into the cities, seeking better schools, better jobs, better health care—in short, a better life. What lessons can be drawn from a broad look at what has been happening in urban America over the last fifty years?

Lesson 1: The real city is the total metropolitan area—city and suburb.

At the end of World War II, urban America was still the inner cities. There were hardly any outer cities. The suburban movement was just starting. The country's biggest cities were booming and bursting at the seams. Drawn by the war industries, millions had left farms and small towns to pack into the cities.

In 1950 almost 70 percent of the population of 168 metropolitan areas lived in 193 central cities. (For an explanation of Census Bureau terms, see Box 1.1.) City residents attended the same city school system. They used the city parks and libraries. They rode city buses, streetcars, and subways to blue- and white-collar jobs within the city or, occasionally, to nearby factories. They fought for control of the same city hall. Although there were often fierce conflicts among ethnic and racial groups, common public institutions were unifying forces (except in the segregated South).

Today the situation is reversed. By 2000 over 60 percent of the population of 331 metropolitan areas lived in suburbs. Equally as important, suburbs no longer simply served as bedroom communities for workers with city-based jobs. By 2000 a majority of jobs in metro areas were located in suburbs as well.

Box 1.1 What Is a Metropolitan Area?

According to the U.S. Census Bureau, a metropolitan area (Metropolitan Statistical Area, MSA, or metro area) is "a geographic area consisting of a large population nucleus together with adjacent communities which have a high degree of economic and social integration with that nucleus." In short, a metro area is a city and its suburbs.

Each metro area must include a central city that, with contiguous, densely settled territory, constitutes a Census Bureau-defined urbanized area of at least 50,000 people. If the largest city has fewer than 50,000 people, the area must have a total population of at least 100,000.

In 1910 the Census Bureau first introduced metropolitan districts. Since then it has used many different methodologies to define metro areas, but by 1950 it had settled on using entire counties as the building blocks of metro areas. Counties outside the central county in which the central city is located are added based on commuting patterns of workers into the central city or the central county.

In recent decades the Census Bureau has recognized additional central cities beyond the historic focal points of many metro areas. Now there are 541 central cities in 331 metro areas. A metro area's title may include up to three central cities, such as "Tampa-St. Petersburg-Clearwater FL MSA."

Eighteen of the largest urban regions are designated as Consolidated Metropolitan Statistical Areas (CMSAs) composed of two or more Primary Metropolitan Statistical Areas (PMSAs). In New England (where counties are not primary local governments), the Census Bureau for statistical purposes has also designated New England County Metropolitan Areas (NECMAs).

In this book the basic unit of analysis is a MSA or PMSA. In metro areas of more than one central city, only the first named city is treated as the central city (for example, Tampa for Tampa-St. Petersburg-Clearwater, Florida).

All metro areas are analyzed as they were defined as of June 30, 1999. A metro area's population in 1950 will include the populations in 1950 of all counties considered part of the metro area in 2000 rather than how the metro area was defined under 1950 conditions.

The traditional city no longer is considered the place to be for families seeking a better life. In fact, housing, jobs, schools, and services are worse in many central cities than they are in the neighboring suburbs. Any attack on urban social and economic problems must treat suburb and city as indivisible parts of a whole.

Lesson 2: Most of America's blacks, Hispanics, and Asians live in urban areas.

Fifty years ago the country's 15 million blacks were still substantially rural and southern, although a tremendous migration into cities north and south had been under way since the Great Depression. Similarly, many of the country's Hispanics were scattered in small towns and cities located largely throughout the Southwest. Asian Americans, always an urban people, were heavily concentrated in West Coast cities.

In 1950 America's population was about 86 to 87 percent white and 13 to 14 percent minority (including Native Americans).[1] Fifty years later America is 31 percent minority, and almost 90 percent of all minorities live in metropolitan areas. In fact, a majority of all blacks, Hispanics, and Asians lives in just thirty metropolitan areas.[2]

Today minorities as well as opportunity are concentrated in urban areas. Social and economic equality can be achieved only through what happens in urban areas.

Lesson 3: Since World War II, urban growth has been low-density, suburban style.

The 1950 census was the high watermark for most of America's big cities. Of the twelve largest cities, ten (all except New York and Los Angeles) hit their population peaks in the 1950 census.

Thereafter, Washington, Wall Street, Detroit, Hollywood, and Madison Avenue made middle-class families an offer they could not refuse: a redefined American Dream. Sustained economic growth, cheap home mortgages, affordable automobiles, and federally subsidized highways—all touted on screens large and small—made that dream house with its own yard, quiet neighborhood, local school, and nearby shopping possible for millions of families. Compared with staying put in many city neighborhoods, suburbia was a bargain. Urban America became Suburban America.

Everyone knows this. What is not always recognized is how universal this pattern has been in postwar America.

The Census Bureau defines "urbanized areas" as the urbanized core of metropolitan areas—the central city and its contiguous, built-up suburbs. Let us focus briefly on urbanized areas as another way to measure the march of suburbanization.

In 1950, 69 million people lived in 157 urbanized areas that covered 12,715 square miles. By 2000, those same 157 urbanized areas contained 155 million residents in 52,388 square miles of developed land—about double the population occupying more than four times as much land. Though many cities had expanded their boundaries, more than 75 percent of the newly developed land and more than 80 percent of the added population were located in suburbs outside central cities.

Population density measures how many people live in a given square mile. Suburbanization cut the population density of these 157 urbanized areas almost in half from 5,391 persons per square mile in 1950 to 2,949 persons per square mile in 2000.

In only ten of the 157 urbanized areas did population density increase. All ten began the postwar period far below the average density, and eight experienced substantial Hispanic immigration.[3]

Within central cities, population density declined as well. In 1950, for example, there were 34 cities with densities of 10,000 or more persons per square mile. Over the next 50 years all of these cities except New York City lost density. By 2000 there were only 14 cities with densities of 10,000 or more persons per square mile.

Three cities had joined the high-density list. Miami and Miami Beach were centers of Cuban, Caribbean, and Central American immigration; Hispanics were 66 and 53 percent of their residents by 2000.

The Pacific Rim's Ellis Island was the greater Los Angeles area, as Hispanic and Asian immigrants filled up Southern California. Hispanic immigration tripled, for example, Santa Ana's density to over 12,000 residents per square mile.

Immigration also focused on the greater New York area, the traditional port of entry (Box 1.2). By 2000 Hispanic and Asian immigrants had lifted New York City to over 8,000,000 residents (its highest population ever). In short, the only cities in America that swam against the suburban stream were cities swimming with the immigrant stream. A certain natural clustering of new immigrants, large families (including extended families), low incomes, and a degree of anti-Hispanic or anti-Asian discrimination in neighboring communities combined to pack immigrants into port-of-entry cities. Everywhere else, most middle-class white Americans for the past fifty years have chosen to raise young families in low-density subdivisions rather than high-density city neighborhoods.

Lesson 4: For a city's population to grow, the city must be elastic.

Think of a city as a map drawn on a rubber sheet. If there is a great deal of vacant land within existing city limits, that city's population density is low. In effect, the rubber sheet map is slack. The city has room for new population growth by filling in undeveloped land. Facing growth opportunities, the city is still elastic within its boundaries because it can in-fill undeveloped land.

On the other hand, what if the city is already densely populated? There is little or no vacant land to develop. Its rubber sheet map is stretched taut within its existing boundaries.

Most high-density cities do not become denser. Typically, a high-density city's growth strategy is to expand its boundaries. It must stretch the edges of its rubber sheet map to take in new territory. It must become more elastic outward rather than upward.

The most common method by which a city acquires new territory is annexation. Sometimes, a city annexes undeveloped land. Often, annexation brings in relatively new, unincorporated subdivisions and commercial areas.

Stretching the edges of the municipal map often creates tension—outside resistance from those to be annexed and inside resistance from a city's current residents. Annexation is not always easy.

How much did cities utilize each mechanism—filling in vacant land and annexing additional territory? Only about 25 percent of all cities actually increased their densities. For many other cities, however, in-fill development was combined with boundary expansion, which often tended to mask the degree of in-fill development.

Box 1.2 New York City, 1790–2000

My analysis has focused on different cities' elasticity amid metro growth over the past fifty years, but all cities were elastic in their youth. New York City serves as a historical microcosm for urban development patterns.

In 1790 the city of New York, located on the tip of Manhattan Island, was the country's largest city, surpassing Philadelphia, Boston, and Baltimore. It had 33,131 residents. Barely 16,000 people were scattered in villages and farms in the surrounding counties (about 50 people per square mile).

By 1890 the city of New York had packed 1.4 million residents onto Manhattan Island (New York County). Linked to the city of New York by the Brooklyn Bridge, the city of Brooklyn in Kings County was the Phoenix of the nineteenth century, increasing its population twenty-fold between 1840 and 1890. The other surrounding counties (Bronx, Queens, and Richmond), however, were still relatively lightly populated.

In 1897 New York's state legislature created the modern New York City by consolidating the five counties as boroughs of the new city and abolishing all municipal governments, including the city of Brooklyn, the nation's seventh most populous city. This legislative act, approved over fierce lobbying opposition from wealthy suburbanites in Brooklyn, created the world's largest city (3.4 million in 1900) and the country's first metropolitan government.

Packed with new European immigrants, the old city of New York (Manhattan) had been approaching its capacity. Manhattan would still grow another 23 percent in population but would peak out by 1910. Consolidation made the city of New York elastic again, above all through acquiring more than 200 square miles of lightly settled land in the Bronx, Queens, and Staten Island.

For the next fifty years much of New York City's suburban growth occurred within its own city limits. Brooklyn grew another 135 percent to its 1950 peak population of 2.7 million. The Bronx grew 625 percent (to 1.5 million) before flattening out after 1950. Queens grew 1,200 percent, reaching 2.0 million by 1970. Decade by decade, Staten Island's farms gave way to subdivisions. These earlier suburbs may have been subway-and-trolley suburbs rather than the auto-based suburbs of the postwar decades, but they were suburbs all the same.

During the 1990s, accelerated immigration from Asia and Latin America lifted the populations of Queens, Staten Island, and New York City as a whole (8,008,278) to all-time highs. Manhattan Island, the original central city, however, had lost—34 percent of its 1910 peak population.

When the Census Bureau in 1910 conceived of metropolitan districts, it designated New York City as the hub of a region including northern New Jersey (Newark and Jersey City) and Westchester County. New York City constituted over 80 percent of the population of this region. By 1950 New York City was still 61 percent of the region's population.

Thereafter, the suburban movement exploded beyond New York's city limits. Between 1950 and 1960 Nassau and Suffolk counties doubled to 2.0 million people. By 2000, Fairfield County, Connecticut, also doubled to 1.0 million, drawing off many of Manhattan's richest executives and corporate headquarters. Commuting patterns extended the greater New York area far down into central New Jersey where the population tripled.

For five decades, while New York City was largely its own suburbs, it was one of America's most successful urban communities. New York City's schools, hospitals, and city services were among the best. With all of its warts, New York City was a great magnet for those seeking a better life—and it largely delivered!

But 1950 was the watershed. From 1900 to 1950, New York City captured over 50 percent of its suburban growth; after 1950, thanks to the immigrant wave of the 1990s, the city has only broken even. By 2000, New York City accounted for less than 38 percent of its regional population.

When it was truly a metro government, New York City was enormously successful. When it slipped into being the central city of a metropolitan region expanding far beyond its borders, its serious social and fiscal problems began.

How elusive regional solutions are for this megaregion, with 21 million residents across 10,166 square miles reaching into four states, is well documented in an excellent book, *Regionalism and Realism,* by Richard Nathan and Gerald Benjamin (Brookings Institution Press, 2001). Their perceptive analysis also illustrates how difficult it is for state and local government leaders to think—and act—outside the "boxes."

Boundary expansion contributed most to municipal elasticity. Between 1950 and 2000 almost four-fifths of the 521 central cities expanded their boundaries by 10 percent or more.[4] The municipal expansion champion was Anchorage, Alaska. By absorbing its entire surrounding borough, the city of Anchorage grew from 12.5 square miles to 1,697.7 square miles (13,482 percent)! Overall, the 521 central cities expanded from 10,360 square miles to 30,699 square miles (196 percent, or 181 percent if Anchorage's massive land grab is discounted).

On the threshold of the era of the suburban lifestyle, the cities with the greatest elasticity had vacant city land to develop *and* the political and legal tools to annex new land. These I will call elastic cities. At the other end of the spectrum were the inelastic cities—typically, older cities already built out at higher than average densities and, for a variety of reasons, unable or unwilling to expand their city limits.

This concept of a city's elasticity is the central idea of this book. Why have some cities been elastic and others have not? What are the demographic, economic, social, and fiscal consequences of inelasticity? If being an elastic city is essential to economic, social, and fiscal health, what can be done to make inelastic cities elastic again or, at least, to benefit as if they were elastic?

Summary data for all 331 metro areas support the first four lessons I have presented. The succeeding lessons are based on analysis of 119 large metro areas but in this chapter are illustrated by contrasting specific metro areas that I have paired: Detroit-Houston, Columbus-Cleveland, Nashville-Louisville, Indianapolis-Milwaukee Albuquerque-Syracuse, Madison-Harrisburg, and Raleigh-Richmond. At first glance several of the metro areas paired may seem to have nothing in common. All pairs, however, have been matched in terms of two key characteristics.

First, from 1950 to 2000 the metro areas in each pair had to house roughly equivalent numbers of new-home occupants (Table 1.1). Since household sizes have fallen throughout America (except in cities with recent immigration), any additional population must be accommodated by building new housing, typically in new subdivisions. For an elastic area (Houston or Columbus, for example) new-home occupants is the same as net metro population growth. For an inelastic area, however, new

TABLE 1.1
EACH PAIR OF METRO AREAS HAD ABOUT THE
SAME NUMBER OF NEW-HOME OCCUPANTS

Metro area	New-home occupants 1950–2000
Houston, Tex.	3,268,824
Detroit, Mich.	2,120,593
Columbus, Ohio	832,042
Cleveland, Ohio	927,845
Nashville, Tenn.	729,403
Louisville, Ky.	531,362
Indianapolis, Ind.	776,453
Milwaukee, Wis.	630,880
Albuquerque, N. Mex.	532,146
Syracuse, N.Y.	270,144
Madison, Wis.	257,169
Harrisburg, Pa.	271,289
Raleigh, N.C.	792,778
Richmond, Va.	568,694

homes must be provided for newcomers to the metro area *and* for current residents moving from the city to the suburbs. For an inelastic area, net metro population growth *and the central city's net loss of population* are added together to calculate new-home occupants. (For an inelastic area, new-home occupants are identical to suburban population growth. I have resisted, however, labeling new-home occupants "suburban growth" because city and suburb potentially competed to house that population.)

The second factor used to pair up metro areas was racial composition. By 2000 the metro areas of each pair had roughly equivalent percentages of black population (Table 1.2).[5]

Although the metro areas in each pair are equivalent in new-home occupants and percentage of black population, the relative elasticity of the principal central cities in each pair is not the same. The more elastic city is listed first; the less elastic city is listed second.[6] (For example, Houston is more elastic than Detroit.)

TABLE 1.2
EACH PAIR OF METRO AREAS HAD ABOUT THE SAME
PERCENTAGE OF BLACKS IN THE POPULATION IN 2000

Metro area	Percentage of blacks in the metro population, 2000
Houston, Tex.	18%
Detroit, Mich.	23
Columbus, Ohio	14
Cleveland, Ohio	19
Nashville, Tenn.	16
Louisville, Ky.	14
Indianapolis, Ind.	14
Milwaukee, Wis.	16
Albuquerque, N. Mex.	3
Syracuse, N.Y.	7
Madison, Wis.	5
Harrisburg, Pa.	8
Raleigh, N.C.	23
Richmond, Va.	31

Lesson 5: Almost all metro areas have grown.

It is easy to label Detroit and Syracuse as "declining Frost Belt areas" and Houston and Albuquerque as "booming Sun Belt areas." The truth is, however, that the populations of Frost Belt areas as well as Sun Belt areas grew as *total metropolitan areas.* In fact, the populations of most metropolitan areas grew over the past five decades.

Table 1.3 presents the metro population growth of the seven pairs of metro areas. Metro areas containing elastic cities have had higher growth rates than metro areas with inelastic cities. These metro areas began at lower population levels. However, in 2000 the metro areas containing the inelastic cities were still somewhat more populous (with the exceptions of Nashville, Indianapolis, and Raleigh, which had edged ahead of Louisville, Milwaukee, and Richmond). The inelastic areas began at much higher population levels and added to that larger base.

TABLE 1.3
ALMOST ALL METRO AREAS HAVE GROWN

Metro area	Metro population		Percentage Change 1950–2000	Percentage Change in 1990s
	1950	2000		
Houston, Tex.	908,822	4,177,646	360%	26%
Detroit, Mich.	3,245,981	4,441,551	37	4
Columbus, Ohio	728,802	1,540,157	111	12
Cleveland, Ohio	1,611,269	2,250,871	40	2
Nashville, Tenn.	501,908	1,231,311	145	25
Louisville, Ky.	628,644	1,025,598	63	5
Indianapolis, Ind.	727,122	1,607,486	121	16
Milwaukee, Wis.	1,014,211	1,500,741	48	5
Albuquerque, N. Mex.	180,592	712,738	295	21
Syracuse, N.Y.	465,114	732,117	57	−1
Madison, Wis.	169,357	426,526	152	16
Harrisburg, Pa.	398,706	629,401	58	7
Raleigh, N.C.	395,163	1,187,941	201	39
Richmond, Va.	463,064	996,512	115	15

Growth rates, of course, are a function of how much is added to how large an initial base. Each additional resident contributes to a higher rate of growth for a smaller initial population base than for a larger initial population base. Thus, the rates of population growth among elastic areas (111 percent to 360 percent) were much higher than growth rates among inelastic areas (37 percent to 115 percent).

Do great disparities in rates of population growth make a difference? Of course they do. For an area to double its population (Columbus, Nashville, Indianapolis, Madison), triple its population (Raleigh-Durham), or even quadruple its population (Houston, Albuquerque) creates a more expansive business and community climate—even a boom town psychology—than exists in an area that grows more slowly.

However, the spectacular rates of population growth of some metro areas have obscured the fact that less spectacularly expanding areas added hundreds of thousands of new residents. For example, from 1950 to 2000 the Houston metro area added 3.3 million people (net), but the Detroit metro area added 1.2

million people (net) as well. Moreover, metro Houston's and metro Detroit's growth were much closer in terms of numbers of families looking for new homes—the key to how local jurisdictions grow within the same metro area.

Lesson 6: Low-density cities can grow through in-fill; high-density cities cannot.

What was the situation of our sample cities in 1950 as the American Dream picked up momentum? The average density for all 521 central cities in 1950 was 5,657 persons per square mile. Albuquerque and Houston were well below the national average (Table 1.4). They would have accommodated some additional growth within existing city limits. Nashville might have had a little room at the inn as well. But even Raleigh, Richmond, and

TABLE 1.4
LOW-DENSITY CITIES CAN GROW THROUGH IN-FILL
HIGH-DENSITY CITIES CANNOT

	City density (persons per square mile) 1950	City density as a percentage of national average city density, 1950
Houston, Tex.	3,726	66%
Detroit, Mich.	13,249	234
Columbus, Ohio	9,541	169
Cleveland, Ohio	12,197	216
Nashville, Tenn.	4,333	77
Louisville, Ky.	9,251	164
Indianapolis, Ind.	7,739	137
Milwaukee, Wis.	12,745	225
Albuquerque, N. Mex.	2,021	36
Syracuse, N.Y.	8,719	154
Madison, Wis.	6,237	110
Harrisburg, Pa.	14,213	251
Raleigh, N.C.	5,971	106
Richmond, Va.	6,208	110

Madison appeared by 1950 to have exceeded the densities associated with the emerging American Dream.

No lower-density city after 1950 expanded beyond 5,000 persons per square mile except for 8 cities with major Hispanic and Asian immigration (6 in California) and three booming college towns—Annapolis (U.S. Naval Academy), Davis (University of California), and State College (Penn State).[7] If city planners in 1950 had had crystal balls, they would have foreseen that any city with a density of 5,000 or more persons per square mile would have to look for more land, more immigrants, or more college students in order to add to its population.

Lesson 7: Elastic cities expand their city limits; inelastic cities do not.

Elastic cities did not just fill up vacant areas within existing city limits. They expanded their city limits greatly (Table 1.5). Houston, Columbus, Albuquerque, Madison, and Raleigh grew through aggressive annexation of surrounding areas. After their earlier pace of annexation had slowed, Nashville and Indianapolis expanded dramatically by consolidating with their home counties, becoming unified governments.

By contrast, almost without exception, inelastic cities entered the postwar growth era locked within their existing boundaries. The city limits of Detroit and Syracuse did not budge. The city of Cleveland added only two square miles, as did the city of Harrisburg. (Harrisburg's proportional growth, adding roughly one-third to its 6.3 square miles, might look significant, but the effect was minuscule within a 1,991-square-mile metro area.) After earlier annexations, Milwaukee and Richmond are now landlocked. Louisville broke out of its jurisdictional straightjacket by consolidating with Jefferson County in January 2003 (Box 3.7).

Why were some cities so elastic and other cities very inelastic?

Lesson 8: Bad state laws can hobble cities.

Constitutionally, local governments are the creatures of state government. State laws differ concerning the power they give municipalities to expand. In New England, for example, the po-

TABLE 1.5
ELASTIC CITIES EXPAND THEIR CITY LIMITS;
INELASTIC CITIES DO NOT

Central city	City area (square miles)		Percentage change	
	1950	2000	1950–2000	1990s
Houston, Tex.	160	579	262%	7%
Detroit, Mich.	139	139	0	0
Columbus, Ohio	39	210	434	10
Cleveland, Ohio	75	78	3	1
Nashville, Tenn.	22	473	2051	0
Louisville, Ky.	40	62	56	0
Indianapolis, Ind.	55	361	555	0
Milwaukee, Wis.	50	96	92	0
Albuquerque, N. Mex.	48	181	277	37
Syracuse, N.Y.	25	25	0	0
Madison, Wis.	15	69	346	19
Harrisburg, Pa.	6	8	29	0
Raleigh, N.C.	11	115	942	30
Richmond, Va.	37	60	62	0

litical map has long been set in stone (in some cases, since colonial times). New England state laws do not even provide for municipal annexation. Similarly, municipal boundaries in New York, New Jersey, and Pennsylvania have been frozen for decades. Elsewhere, state statutes often attach conditions that can severely limit a municipality's practical ability to annex additional territory. Annexation may be allowed only upon voluntary petition by property owners. Often an affirmative vote of affected landowners is required (or even approval by voters in the annexing municipality).

Table 1.6 summarizes a 1971 study of different cities' annexation powers and constraints. Raleigh's continuous expansion was guaranteed by North Carolina's liberal annexation laws; it had the power—even the obligation—to annex urbanizing areas regardless of property owners' desires. Texas also allowed cities such as Houston to annex unincorporated areas by unilateral council action. Albuquerque's annexations had to be unanimously approved by affected property owners, but the economics of city water and sewer services motivated large land developers to seek annexation.

By the mid-1960s, shortly after Harrisburg added less than two square miles, Pennsylvania nullified its annexation laws; cities can expand now only through formal mergers (which rarely happens). Kentucky's laws were pro-annexation, but also provided a poison pill—ready self-incorporation of small subdivisions facing annexation. After ninety-three suburban micromunicipalities had been organized, Louisville negotiated a moratorium on both annexations and new incorporations in return for a tax-sharing compact with Jefferson County. In 1979 the Virginia General Assembly insulated urban counties from further annexations by what it designated as independent cities such as Richmond.

Lesson 9: Neighbors can trap cities.

Regardless of annexation laws, in all states, one municipality cannot annex property within another municipality, regardless of the disparity in size. Typically, this is the most insurmountable barrier to annexations by a central city. Thus, many older cities became gradually surrounded by smaller cities, towns, and villages. Newer central cities often faced only farmland, swamp, or sagebrush.

Table 1.7 shows the elbow room each of the target cities had. In 1950 no city came close to filling up its home county; central cites covered only from 1 percent to only 23 percent of home-county land area. Detroit, nevertheless, was bounded by the Detroit River (an international boundary) and by fifteen municipalities enclosing 75 percent of its city limits. Cleveland was completely hemmed in by Lake Erie on the north and by twenty smaller municipalities ringing its city limits. Regardless of state laws, Detroit and Cleveland had nowhere to grow. By contrast, Columbus annexed aggressively, driven by two strategic goals: to become the most populous city in Ohio and never to allow itself to become completely surrounded by incorporated suburbs.

After Milwaukee almost doubled its territory by annexation in the 1950s, all remaining townships in Milwaukee County converted themselves into annexation-proof municipalities. Within the same state, however, Madison was able to slow down the

TABLE 1.6
BAD STATE LAWS CAN HOBBLE CITIES

	Municipal annexation			Approval by voters		
	Authorized by state law	Begun by property owner petition	Begun by city council action	Within annexed area	Within annexing city	Approval by county government
Houston, Tex.	Yes	Yes	Yes	No	No	No
Detroit, Mich.	Yes	Yes	[No]	[Yes]	[Yes]	No
Columbus, Ohio	Yes	Yes	Yes	[Yes]	No	[Yes]
Cleveland, Ohio	Yes	Yes	Yes	[Yes]	No	[Yes]
Nashville, Tenn.	Yes	Yes	Yes	[Yes]	[Yes]	No
Louisville, Ky.	Yes	No	Yes	No	No	No
Indianapolis, Ind.	Yes	Yes	Yes	No	No	No
Milwaukee, Wis.	Yes	Yes	[No]	[Yes]	No	No
Albuquerque, N. Mex.	Yes	Yes	Yes	[Yes]	No	No
Syracuse, N.Y.	Yes*	Yes	[No]	[Yes]	No	No
Madison, Wis.	Yes	Yes	Yes	[Yes]	No	No
Harrisburg, Pa.	No	n/a	n/a	n/a	n/a	n/a
Raleigh, N.C.	Yes	Yes	Yes	No	No	No
Richmond, Va.	Yes#	Yes	Yes	No	No	[Yes]

Note: Adverse requirements are highlighted by brackets
* New York annexation law effectively nullified by state constitutional amendment requiring voter approval of boundary changes.
# Virginia annexation law rendered moot by legislature's requiring county approval in 1979.

TABLE 1.7
ELASTIC CITIES HAD ELBOW ROOM TO GROW; INELASTIC CITIES DID NOT

	Home county	City area as a percentage of home county area 1950	City area as a percentage of home county area 2000	Percentage of city limits enclosed by other municipalities 1950	Number of other municipalities in home county 1990	Number of townships in home county 1990
Houston, Tex.	Harris	9%	33%	10%	27	0
Detroit, Mich.	Wayne	23	23	75	33	[10]
Columbus, Ohio	Franklin	7	39	15	24	17
Cleveland, Ohio	Cuyahoga	17	17	100	55	4
Nashville, Tenn.	Davidson	4	94	1	6	0
Louisville, Ky.	Jefferson	10	16	30	94	0
Indianapolis, Ind.	Marion	14	91	25	15	9
Milwaukee, Wis.	Milwaukee	21	40	25	19	0
Albuquerque, N. Mex.	Bernalillo	4	16	0	2	0
Syracuse, N.Y.	Onondaga	3	3	100	16	[19]
Madison, Wis.	Dane	1	6	20	24	34
Harrisburg, Pa.	Dauphin	1	1	100	17	[23]
Raleigh, N.C.	Wake	1	14	0	12	0
Richmond, Va.	Independent city	na	na	0	na	na

Note: Townships with municipal status are highlighted by brackets.

municipalization of its local townships. (Townships will be discussed in chapter III and Box 3.6.)

Houston, Albuquerque, and Raleigh had relatively clear sailing in terms of implementing their annexation strategies.

Lesson 10: Old cities are complacent; young cities are ambitious.

Certainly one clear distinction between elastic and inelastic cities is age; elastic cities are younger than inelastic cities. Table 1.8 lists the census at which each city first exceeded 100,000 inhabitants.

On average the inelastic cities passed 100,000 or more residents around 1890, while the elastic cities did not reach that milestone until about 1930. An average of 1930, however, masks an important difference: Houston, Columbus, Nashville, and Indianapolis passed the 100,000 mark only a decade or two after the inelastic cities did; Albuquerque, Madison, and Raleigh are truly recent entrants to big city status.

TABLE 1.8
INELASTIC CITIES ARE OLDER THAN ELASTIC CITIES

	Census when the population exceeded 100,000
Houston, Tex.	1920
Detroit, Mich.	1880
Columbus, Ohio	1900
Cleveland, Ohio	1880
Nashville, Tenn.	1910
Louisville, Ky.	1870
Indianapolis, Ind.	1890
Milwaukee, Wis.	1880
Albuquerque, N. Mex.	1960
Syracuse, N.Y.	1900
Madison, Wis.	1970
Harrisburg, Pa.	1920*
Raleigh, N.C.	1970
Richmond, Va.	1910

*Census when the population exceeded 50,000

What transformed the futures of Houston, Columbus, Nashville, and Indianapolis was, in large measure, the attitude of their community leadership (with citizen support). Houston and Columbus were expansionist through aggressive annexation (despite limitations on their legal powers). Even more striking, the leadership of Nashville and Indianapolis transformed their communities by successful city-county consolidations. Without city-county consolidation, which lifted both cities out of slow erosion, Nashville and Indianapolis would probably be not much different from Louisville and Milwaukee.

On the eve of the suburban era, older, established cities tended to be complacent. Already centers of national or regional wealth, they focused on dividing up the pie rather than on making the pie larger. By 1950 the shift of people, jobs, and power to the suburbs was under way. A failure of initiative from within as well as legal, historical, and political constraints from without contributed to making many older cities inelastic.

By contrast, younger cities were on the make as they entered the postwar era. Certainly, many would benefit from macroeconomic changes (for example, the growth of industry in the Sun Belt). Many would even benefit from technological changes (for example, inexpensive air conditioning units for Sun Belt homes and offices). But many cities made their own futures by willing their own elasticity.

Lesson 11: Racial prejudice has shaped growth patterns.

Both racial prejudice and discriminatory public policies played a major role in the evolution of overwhelmingly white suburbs surrounding increasingly black and Hispanic inelastic cities (see Box 1.3 on red-lining minority neighborhoods).

Certainly some new suburbanites were motivated by nonracial considerations. Many middle-class families moved because older cities lacked dream houses at affordable prices in good neighborhoods with good schools. Others moved to flee high city taxes and low city politics or to live nearer their suburban jobs.

Yet in many metro areas, racially motivated white flight was undeniably a major factor. "Good" neighborhoods with "good" schools often were seen as neighborhoods and schools without any blacks and, to a lesser degree, without any Hispanics. After the civil rights revolution in the 1960s, neighborhoods and

Box 1.3 Federal Government Segregated Suburbs

"For Whites Only" was the sign that the federal government hung out as America's suburbs exploded with millions of new families in the postwar decades. The federal government did not create discrimination in America's housing markets, but it institutionalized it on an unprecedented scale.[1]

In 1933, as millions of owners were losing their homes during the Great Depression, the New Deal created the Home Owners' Loan Corporation (HOLC). To help struggling families meet mortgage payments, HOLC offered low-interest, long-term mortgage loans. HOLC developed a ratings system to evaluate the risks associated with loans made to specific urban neighborhoods. HOLC designated four categories of neighborhood risk; on its "residential security maps" the highest risk areas were colored red. Black neighborhoods were always coded red and were "redlined"; even those with small black percentages were usually rated as "hazardous" and residents were denied loans.

HOLC's loan program was small, but the impact of its discriminatory practices was enormous. During the 1930s and 1940s, HOLC residential security maps were widely used by private banks for their own loan practices. When the Federal Housing Administration (1937) and the Veterans Administration (1944) were founded, they embraced HOLC's underwriting practices. The 1939 FHA *Underwriting Manual,* for example, stated that "if a neighborhood is to retain stability, it is necessary that the properties shall continue to be occupied by the same social and racial classes."

FHA and VA largely financed the rapid suburbanization of the United States after World War II. The federal government's regulations favored construction of single-family homes but discour-

schools without *poor* blacks and Hispanics increasingly satisfied the "good" test.

Having escaped so-called city problems, most suburbanites vigorously resisted city annexation, often by incorporating their new communities. More recently, many city blacks and Hispanics—finally taking control of City Hall—also resisted city expansion, especially where past annexations had been instruments of maintaining white control (Box 1.4).

History, geography, state laws, civic leadership (or lack of same), and racial attitudes all shaped the elasticity or inelastic-

aged the building of multifamily apartments. As a result, the vast majority of FHA and VA mortgages went to new, white, middle-class suburban neighborhoods, and very few were awarded to black neighborhoods in central cities. Historian Kenneth Jackson found that from 1934 to 1960 suburban St. Louis County received six times as much FHA mortgage money per capita as did the city of St. Louis. Per capita FHA lending in suburban Long Island was eleven times greater than in Brooklyn and sixty times greater than in the Bronx.

Such government practices died hard. As late as 1950, FHA was still encouraging the use of restrictive racial covenants two years after the U.S. Supreme Court had ruled them unconstitutional. FHA's red-lining continued overtly until the mid-1960s, when Robert Weaver became the first African American HUD secretary. The weak Civil Rights Act of 1968 finally outlawed housing discrimination. However, the full extent of discrimination in mortgage lending was only revealed after passage of the Home Mortgage Disclosure Act (1975), and significant mortgage funds began to flow back into inner-city neighborhoods only with vigorous enforcement of the Community Reinvestment Act (1977).

Extreme segregation of America's housing markets was not the result of some natural process of self-segregation. For decades it was force-fed by discriminatory rules of the game from federal, state, and local governments.

1. This discussion is adapted from Douglas S. Massey and Nancy A. Denton, *American Apartheid: Segregation and the Making of the Underclass* (Cambridge, Mass.: Harvard University Press, 1993), ch. 2, which in turn cites extensively from Kenneth T. Jackson, *Crabgrass Frontier: The Suburbanization of the United States* (Cambridge: Oxford University Press, 1985).

ity of cities. What were the demographic, social, economic, and fiscal consequences of being an inelastic vs. an elastic city?

Lesson 12: Elastic cities capture suburban growth; inelastic cities contribute to suburban growth.

Postwar growth has been primarily suburban style, low-density development emphasizing detached, single-family homes. At the outset of the postwar period elastic cities had large inventories of

---

Box 1.4 Annexation and Federal Voting Rights Act

Since 1971, a new hurdle has existed for many municipalities' annexation powers—the federal Voting Rights Act.

Under section 5, municipalities in all or portions of twenty-nine states with large black, Hispanic, or Native American populations are required to clear proposed annexations with the U.S. Department of Justice. The federal concern is that by annexing predominantly white outlying areas, municipalities would dilute the growing political strength of blacks and Hispanics.

In actuality, the Justice Department typically objects to less than 2 percent of all annexations submitted for review. Of these questioned annexations, less than 1 percent is ultimately prevented by either Justice Department objections or the federal courts. Many contested annexations are resolved by changing the political system to enhance minority representation, typically by shifting from at-large to districted local elections.

Perhaps the most famous and bitterly contested annexation was Richmond's annexation of twenty-three square miles of Chesterfield County in 1970. For seven years thereafter, federal courts blocked further city elections until the case was finally decided by the U.S. Supreme Court.

Opponents charged that by annexing over 47,000 new residents (97 percent white), the white-dominated Richmond city council had sought to dilute growing black political power. Proponents argued that the annexation's purpose was to strengthen Richmond's middle-class population, acquire vacant land for residential, commercial, and industrial growth, and expand the tax base to meet Richmond's future revenue needs.

The irony is that both sides were correct. By unanimous vote, the U.S. Supreme Court ruled in 1975 that the annexation "was infected by the impermissible purpose of denying the right to vote based on race."[1] The court allowed the annexation to stand,

---

undeveloped land or would be able to annex either undeveloped land or new subdivisions. They captured much of this suburban-style growth within their own municipal boundaries.

Inelastic cities could not grow either through in-fill or annexation. They could not compete with new suburbs in offering the desired suburban-style model for family life. Incapable of capturing a share of suburban-type development, inelastic cities actually contributed white, middle-class families to the new

based on Richmond's shift to a nine-member council elected by wards.

After adding 47,000 new residents (and an estimated one-quarter to its tax base), the 1970 annexation, however, marked the end of Richmond's expansion. Blacks gained a majority of the ward council seats by 1978, electing Henry Marsh as Richmond's first African American mayor.

Richmond's black community has gained political control of a depreciating asset. While the three adjacent counties have more than doubled with 340,000 new residents, Richmond's population has dropped by over 51,000, or –21 percent since 1970. City income growth has steadily lagged behind suburban income growth. City incomes are now 82 percent of suburban incomes. Much of Richmond's black middle class has left the city for suburban locations.

Richmond's annexation powers were ended by the Virginia legislature, which in 1979 exempted urban counties from further annexation without county approval. Probably Richmond's black majority city council would have lost all interest in further annexations in any event in order not to jeopardize its newly acquired political power.

The saga of Richmond's annexation battle epitomizes one of urban America's sad realities. In many cities, achieving political dominance has also trapped large numbers of blacks or Hispanics in cities of declining social and economic opportunity as abandonment of the city by middle-class residents, investors, and employers accelerates.

1. All information on the history of the Richmond annexation dispute is taken from John V. Moeser and Rutledge M. Dennis, *The Politics of Annexation: Oligarchic Power in a Southern City* (Cambridge, Mass.: Schenkman, 1982); quotation on page 172.

suburbs. In recent years in areas such as Washington, D.C., and Atlanta a rapidly growing black middle class has moved to the suburbs as well.

Table 1.9 sums up the effect in terms of a city's capture or contribute percentage. The capture or contribute percentage is calculated by dividing a city's net population growth by the area's new-home occupants. In effect, Table 1.9 measures a city's success or failure in competing for middle-class families with its suburbs.

TABLE 1.9
ELASTIC CITIES CAPTURE SUBURBAN GROWTH;
INELASTIC CITIES CONTRIBUTE TO SUBURBAN GROWTH

	City capture/ contribute percentage 1950–2000	City capture/ contribute percentage in the 1990s
Houston, Tex.	42%	38%
Detroit, Mich.	–42	–30
Columbus, Ohio	40	48
Cleveland, Ohio	–47	–36
Nashville, Tenn.	51	14
Louisville, Ky.	–21	–20
Indianapolis, Ind.	46	18
Milwaukee, Wis.	–6	–45
Albuquerque, N. Mex.	66	52
Syracuse, N.Y.	–27	–165
Madison, Wis.	44	28
Harrisburg, Pa.	–15	–8
Raleigh, N.C.	27	21
Richmond, Va.	–6	–4

Over the past fifty years Houston captured 42 percent of its region's new-home occupants, while Detroit contributed –42 percent of its suburbs' new-home occupants. Columbus captured 40 percent, Cleveland contributed –47 percent, and so forth.[8] (In the original *Cities without Suburbs*, I wrote "Milwaukee and Richmond have broken about even to this point, but are playing out losing hands unless they can radically change their cards." They did not and are now sliding steadily down the list.)

Having used changes in city population implicitly to calculate the capture or contribute percentages, it is time to present explicitly the demographic consequences of elasticity and inelasticity.

Lesson 13: Elastic cities gain population; inelastic cities lose population.

As Table 1.10 makes agonizingly clear, in the Age of Sprawl, inelastic cities suffered catastrophic population losses. Inelastic

TABLE 1.10
ELASTIC CITIES GAIN POPULATION;
INELASTIC CITIES LOSE POPULATION

	City population			
	1950 (or peak*)	2000	Percentage change 1950–2000	1990s
Houston, Tex.	596,163	1,953,631	228%	20%
Detroit, Mich.	1,849,568	951,270	−49	−8
Columbus, Ohio	375,901	711,470	89	12
Cleveland, Ohio	914,808	478,403	−48	−5
Nashville, Tenn.	174,307	545,524	213	7
Louisville, Ky.	390,639	256,231	−34	−5
Indianapolis, Ind.	427,173	781,870	83	7
Milwaukee, Wis.	741,324	596,974	−19	−5
Albuquerque, N. Mex.	96,815	448,607	363	17
Syracuse, N.Y.	220,583	147,306	−33	−10
Madison, Wis.	96,056	208,054	117	9
Harrisburg, Pa.	89,544	48,950	−45	−7
Raleigh, N.C.	65,679	276,093	320	33
Richmond, Va.	249,332	197,790	−21	−3

*Peak population: Louisville and Milwaukee in 1960; Richmond in 1970

cities lost from −19 percent to −49 percent of their inhabitants from their population peaks. Metro population growth occurred entirely in suburbs outside these cities' boundaries. Though some other inelastic cities recovered population from Hispanic or Asian immigration during the 1990s, these particular inelastic cities did not; they lost an average of −6 percent of their inhabitants during the decade.

In sharp contrast, elastic cities grew dramatically. Columbus, Indianapolis, and Madison doubled, Houston and Nashville tripled, and Albuquerque and Raleigh quadrupled their city populations. All continued to grow during the 1990s (four at double-digit rates of increase).

Over the past fifty years, average household size declined about 20 percent in America. Cities that lost about 20 percent of their population also lost households (think: taxpayers, consumers) as well.

Lesson 14: When a city stops growing, it starts shrinking.

In the early postwar period, Milwaukee, Louisville, and Richmond continued to expand in population and in area (by 46, 22, and 23 square miles, respectively). Between 1950 and 1960 Milwaukee almost doubled its area and added over 100,000 new residents (about 16 percent growth). Then, as annexation stopped, Milwaukee peaked out. Since its 1960 peak Milwaukee has lost all of its added population. By 2000, its population was −19 percent below its 1960 peak level.

In similar fashion Louisville and Richmond continued to grow in population while geographic expansion was under way. Then, when geographic expansion halted, their populations began dropping. The drop in Louisville was precipitous (−34 percent, from its 1960 peak), while Richmond's population erosion has been more gradual (−21 percent, from its 1970 peak). Richmond's population is now approaching its 1940 level, while pre-consolidation Louisville had turned its population clock back to the 1920s!

Lesson 15: Inelastic areas are more segregated than elastic areas.

The high concentration of blacks and Hispanics, particularly poor blacks and Hispanics, in inelastic central cities dominated their regions' social geography and shaped decisively the choices that middle-class families (white and black) made about where to live and work. Table 1.11 illustrates the significant differences between inelastic areas and elastic areas in terms of residential segregation of blacks.

Each metropolitan pairing had similar percentages of blacks. Sharply different metro growth patterns yielded sharply different racial populations for central cities.

In 2000 metro Houston, for example, was 18 percent black. Many of its new suburbs lay within Houston's city limits. As a result, the city of Houston was only 25 percent black. Metro Detroit had a somewhat higher black population (23 percent) than did metro Houston. With virtually all postwar subdivisions (to which Detroit's white residents moved) built outside its city lim-

TABLE 1.11
INELASTIC AREAS ARE MORE RACIALLY
SEGREGATED THAN ELASTIC AREAS

Metro area	Percentage black in 2000			Metro segregation index*	Index change 1990s
	Metro area	City	Suburbs		
Houston, Tex.	18%	25%	11%	67	0
Detroit, Mich.	23	82	7	85	−3
Columbus, Ohio	14	25	4	63	−5
Cleveland, Ohio	19	51	10	77	−5
Nashville, Tenn.	16	27	16	57	−4
Louisville, Ky.	14	33	8	64	−6
Indianapolis, Ind.	14	26	2	71	−5
Milwaukee, Wis.	16	37	2	82	−1
Albuquerque, N. Mex.	3	3	2	32	−10
Syracuse, N.Y.	7	25	2	69	−5
Madison, Wis.	5	6	3	46	−5
Harrisburg, Pa.	8	55	4	71	−5
Raleigh, N.C.	23	28	16	46	−3
Richmond, Va.	31	58	21	57	−4

*Segregation Index: Scale 0 to 100 (100 = total apartheid)

its, the city of Detroit was 82 percent black. Houston's black population proportionally was over twice its suburbs' black population (11 percent); Detroit's black population, however, was proportionally almost twelve times its suburbs' black population (7 percent).

One might expect the demographic profile of an elastic city to reflect fairly closely the demographic profile of its metro area, since, by definition, an elastic city encompasses much of its region. However, the metropolitan black segregation index used in the last two columns of Table 1.11 is calculated on a census tract-by-census tract basis as if political boundaries do not exist (Box 1.5). On a scale of 0 to 100 (with 100 = total apartheid), metro Detroit, neighborhood-by-neighborhood, was much more residentially segregated (an index score of 85) than was metro Houston (67) in 2000.

Racial segregation in inelastic areas was consistently higher. Black segregation was always less within an elastic metro area

---

Box 1.5. SUNY-Albany Calculates Segregation

An indispensable resource tracking racial, ethnic, and economic disparities is the Lewis Mumford Center for Comparative Urban and Regional Research at State University of New York at Albany. The center's website (<http://mumford1.dyndns.org/cen2000/data.html>) provides easy-to-view sortable lists and download-able tables calculating various segregation indices for 331 metro areas. Topics covered include segregation of the whole popula-tion, children under 18, Hispanic and Asian groups, school seg-regation, homeowners and renters (by race), new Americans, state of the cities, separate and unequal, and diversity in black and white.

The capsule description of the school segregation tables pre-views their scope: "Ethnic and racial composition data of ele-mentary schools for 1989–90 and 1999–2000, segregation of school children, and indicators of economic disparities including segregation of 'poor' from 'non-poor' children (Dissimilarity In-dex), exposure of poor school children to other poor and non-poor children (Exposure indices), and the percentage of poor children in the school of the average member of a racial/ethnic group." Indices are calculated by metro area, central city, and suburban area but also by school district within each metro area.

For those who do not revel in data, the website also accesses many fascinating reports, such as "Separate and Unequal: The Neighborhood Gap for Blacks and Hispanics in Metropolitan America," "The Muslim World in Metropolitan America," and "Choosing Segregation: Racial Imbalance in American Public Schools, 1990–2000."

---

than it was within its paired inelastic metro area. Between metro areas in different sections of the country (for example, Houston-Detroit, Albuquerque-Syracuse), differences in racial patterns might be explained in terms of broad sectional differences (Sun Belt-Frost Belt, for example). The differences, however, held true between metro areas in the same section (Raleigh-Richmond, Nashville-Louisville) and even within the same state (Colum-bus-Cleveland).

The good news, as indicated in the last column, is that the level of black segregation has been slowly coming down; thirty years ago, for example, most of these regions had black segregation index scores in the eighties and low nineties. The bad news is that for African Americans and other blacks, the level of residential segregation in most regions is still extraordinarily high—far beyond that experienced historically by any immigrant group in the nineteenth and twentieth centuries.

Lesson 16: Major immigration increases Hispanic segregation.

In 2000, Hispanics were significantly less segregated than were blacks (although Hispanic segregation increased in many regions). Typically, the level of Hispanic residential segregation was ten to twenty points below black segregation within the same metro area. In addition, Southwestern communities (typically, elastic regions) generally had many more Hispanics than did other areas of the country. In less elastic areas, however, even small Hispanic populations were usually more segregated (Table 1.12).

Whereas black segregation declined everywhere in the 1990s, Hispanic segregation increased, particularly in metro areas such as Nashville and Raleigh that experienced a sudden influx of Hispanic immigrants. Only in Albuquerque, whose Hispanic ancestors settled New Mexico a generation before the Pilgrims landed on Plymouth Rock, did Hispanic residential segregation decline during the past decade.

Hopefully, higher Hispanic segregation levels will be a temporary phenomenon, reflecting the tendency of new immigrants to band together in port of entry neighborhoods. Where the Hispanic population was relatively stable, residential segregation declined as succeeding generations fanned out into a wider range of communities.

Lesson 17: Highly racially segregated regions are also highly economically segregated regions.

Table 1.13 presents the same segregation index as in tables 1.11 and 1.12 but calculated for all persons who fell below the federally defined poverty line. Economic segregation largely tracked

TABLE 1.12
MAJOR IMMIGRATION INCREASES HISPANIC SEGREGATION

Metro area	Metro Percentage Hispanic		Metro Segregation index*	
	1990	2000	1990	2000
Houston, Tex.	21%	30%	50	56
Detroit, Mich.	2	3	40	46
Columbus, Ohio	1	2	29	38
Cleveland, Ohio	2	3	58	58
Nashville, Tenn.	1	3	25	46
Louisville, Ky.	1	2	27	36
Indianapolis, Ind.	1	3	27	44
Milwaukee, Wis.	4	6	56	60
Albuquerque, N. Mex.	37	42	42	41
Syracuse, N.Y.	1	2	42	46
Madison, Wis.	2	3	30	38
Harrisburg, Pa.	2	3	54	55
Raleigh, N.C.	1	6	25	43
Richmond, Va.	1	2	32	41

*Segregation Index: Scale 0 to 100 (100 = total apartheid)

racial segregation. Inelastic areas were significantly more economically segregated than elastic areas. In fact, Milwaukee, Cleveland, and Detroit were the first, fifth, and sixth most economically segregated metropolitan areas in the country in 2000.

Thus, while barriers based on race have been coming down in regional housing markets, barriers based on income have been going up. Jim Crow by income is replacing Jim Crow by race.

Lesson 18: Inelastic cities have wide income gaps with their suburbs; elastic cities maintain greater city-suburb balance.

Fifty years ago all central cities had about the same median family incomes as their suburbs (Table 1.14). (A median is the midpoint that divides a population into equal halves.) Over the next five decades median family income of all cities except very elastic Albuquerque and Raleigh dropped below suburban levels.

Table 1.13
Highly Racially Segregated Regions Are (also) Highly
Economically Segregated Regions

Metro area	Metro economic segregation index			
	1970	1980	1990	2000
Houston, Tex.	37	36	38	36
Detroit, Mich.	39	44	51	45
Columbus, Ohio	39	41	44	41
Cleveland, Ohio	43	44	49	45
Nashville, Tenn.	37	33	35	34
Louisville, Ky.	38	38	40	40
Indianapolis, Ind.	34	36	40	37
Milwaukee, Wis.	39	46	56	51
Albuquerque, N. Mex.	36	33	35	33
Syracuse, N.Y.	29	35	40	37
Madison, Wis.	28	30	43	na
Harrisburg, Pa.	33	30	38	32
Raleigh, N.C.	na	32	36	34
Richmond, Va.	39	39	45	42

*Segregation index: Scale 0 to 100 (100 = total apartheid)

With so many middle class families having left, however, family incomes in inelastic cities fell far below suburban levels.

The city-to-suburb per capita income percentage is the single most important indicator of an urban area's social health. (Unlike median family income, per capita income reflects incomes of wealthier individuals and single-person households.) Income levels in inelastic cities fall well below suburban levels, ranging from lows for Detroit, Cleveland, and Milwaukee (54, 57, and 58 percent, respectively) to highs for Louisville and Richmond (76 and 82 percent). Elastic cities, however, keep pace better with suburban levels, averaging 89 percent of suburban levels.

During the 1990s, the city-to-suburb per capita income percentage declined somewhat for all elastic cities. In effect, suburbanization was occurring so rapidly that city annexation strategies couldn't keep up. Notably, after decades of precipitous decline, both Detroit and Cleveland rebounded slightly from catastrophically high income gaps. Falling city unemployment rates and modest movement of young professionals and empty

TABLE 1.14
INELASTIC CITIES HAVE WIDE INCOME GAP WITH SUBURBS;
ELASTIC CITIES MAINTAIN GREATER CITY-SUBURB BALANCE

Metro area	City percentage of metro median family income		City percentage of suburban per capita income	
	1950	2000	1990	2000
Houston, Tex.	97%	79%	89%	85%
Detroit, Mich.	99	57	53	54
Columbus, Ohio	98	86	81	81
Cleveland, Ohio	91	58	53	57
Nashville, Tenn.	85	92	98	92
Louisville, Ky.	99	74	79	76
Indianapolis, Ind.	98	89	90	87
Milwaukee, Wis.	97	67	62	58
Albuquerque, N. Mex.	106	102	118	113
Syracuse, N.Y.	100	67	77	71
Madison, Wis.	109	95	95	89
Harrisburg, Pa.	101	57	72	69
Raleigh, N.C.	119	101	103	100
Richmond, Va.	97	68	83	82

nesters back to the city, plus growing lower-income populations in many older, inner suburbs, helped both cities arrest their relative economic decline.

Lesson 19: Poverty is more disproportionately concentrated in inelastic cities than in elastic cities.

What about poverty levels? Historically, the South and West have been lower income regions than the Northeast and Midwest, and today that pattern still persists (Table 1.15). A slightly higher percentage of the population fell below the poverty line in southern and western areas (11.5 percent) than in northeastern and midwestern areas (10 percent). However, poverty was much more concentrated in the inelastic cities (24 percent) than in the elastic cities (14 percent).

TABLE 1.15
POVERTY IS MORE DISPROPORTIONATELY CONCENTRATED
IN INELASTIC CITIES THAN IN ELASTIC CITIES

	Poverty rate in 2000		City fair share of poverty index	City fair share of poverty index
Metro area	Metro	City	2000	1990
Houston, Tex.	13.9%	19.2%	138	137
Detroit, Mich.	10.7	26.1	244	251
Columbus, Ohio	10.1	14.8	147	146
Cleveland, Ohio	10.8	26.3	244	243
Nashville, Tenn.	10.1	13.3	132	119
Louisville, Ky.	11.6	21.6	198	178
Indianapolis, Ind.	8.6	11.9	137	130
Milwaukee, Wis.	10.6	21.3	201	191
Albuquerque, N. Mex.	13.8	13.5	98	96
Syracuse, N.Y.	12.1	27.3	226	218
Madison, Wis.	9.4	15.0	160	153
Harrisburg, Pa.	8.1	24.6	304	346
Raleigh, N.C.	10.2	11.5	113	116
Richmond, Va.	9.3	21.4	230	213

In part, the pattern is sectional. In the South and West, many poor households still live in rural and semi-urban sections of the metro areas. Poverty is both more spread out in the countryside and more dispersed within the urbanized area itself. But concentrated poverty is also the result of cities' inelasticity, which magnifies economic segregation.

A simple measure of disproportionate concentration of poverty in a central city is what I have called a city's fair share of poverty index. The index is the ratio between the city's percentage of poor residents and the total metro area's percentage of poor residents. (A city's fair share would be reflected as an index of 100.)

In 2000, elastic cities were home to only slightly more than their fair share of the metro area poor (average index: 132). By contrast, inelastic cities had over twice their fair share of their regions' poor (average index: 235). At the extremes, Albuquerque had slightly less than its fair share (index: 98) while Harrisburg had three times its fair share of poverty (index: 304).

Lesson 20: Little boxes regions foster segregation; Big Box regions facilitate integration.

"Public policy dictates where development occurs," states the National Association of Home Builders.[10] Local government plans, zoning maps, and investments in public facilities have a major impact on who lives, works, shops, and plays where.

As Table 1.16 shows, local governance in inelastic regions was highly fragmented. The inelastic central cities contained less than one quarter of the regional population (with the exception

TABLE 1.16
LITTLE BOXES REGIONS FOSTER SEGREGATION;
BIG BOX REGIONS FACILITATE INTEGRATION

Metro area	Percentage of area population governed by central city	Number of suburban governments 2002	Segregation index	
			Blacks 2000	Poor 2000
Houston, Tex.	47%	84	67	36
Detroit, Mich.	21	214	85	45
Columbus, Ohio	46	181	63	41
Cleveland, Ohio	21	202	77	45
Nashville, Tenn.	44	49	57	34
Louisville, Ky.	25	126*	64	40
Indianapolis, Ind.	49	87	71	37
Milwaukee, Wis.	40	92	82	51
Albuquerque, N. Mex.	63	14	32	33
Syracuse, N.Y.	20	130	69	37
Madison, Wis.	49	59	46	na
Harrisburg, Pa.	8	129	71	32
Raleigh, N.C.	44	37	46	34
Richmond, Va.	20	13	57	42

*Indiana townships, which do not exercise general governmental powers, are omitted.

of Milwaukee). They were surrounded by a myriad of incorporated, little boxes suburban governments. (With Virginia's unique system of strong county governments and independent cities, metro Richmond was the exception.) Since all net growth was occurring outside the central cities, little boxes suburban governments shaped land development policy.

Elastic regions had more unified governance. The central city was a Big Box where city hall served over 40 percent of the region's inhabitants. (Within its multiple central cities region, Raleigh served 44 percent of Wake County's population.) Elastic cities had relatively fewer suburban governments as rivals and often substantially controlled regional development through annexation and utility policies.

Why should patterns of local governance have any impact on racial and economic segregation? One factor is a local government's sense of constituency. In my experience, the unspoken mission of most little town councils (and most little school boards) is "to keep our town (and our schools) just the way they are for people just like *us*"—whoever "*us*" happens to be. In earlier decades, local policies to keep out the Other could be very overt. In the post–civil rights revolution era, many suburban governments now use planning and zoning powers more subtly. They may require large minimum lot sizes for new homes or ban apartment construction outright, for example, to exclude lower-income households, including many minorities.

Mayors and city councils of elastic, Big Box cities are not all Boy Scouts and Girl Scouts, but they do represent broader, more diverse constituencies. As a result, Big Box governments do not adopt exclusionary policies as readily as do little boxes governments; Big Box mayors and councils are accountable to the very voters that would otherwise be excluded. Governance counts.

The way a metro area is governed was not the only factor affecting integration. Another factor was age. Old cities generally had more decaying neighborhoods in which poor blacks and Hispanics were concentrated. Younger cities emerged in an era of somewhat more enlightened racial attitudes (and some effective civil rights laws).

Does greater socioeconomic integration automatically flow from greater governmental unity? Probably not. What is clear is that, absent federal or state mandates, a metro area in which local government is highly fragmented is usually incapable of adopting broad, integrating strategies. Conversely, a metro area in which key planning and zoning powers are concentrated under a dominant local government has the potential to implement policies to promote greater racial and economic integration if that government has the vision and courage to do so.

Lesson 21: Little boxes school districts foster segregation; Big Box school districts facilitate integration.

Table 1.17 shows that how public education was organized largely paralleled how local governance was organized. The school district serving a central city was typically a region's

TABLE 1.17
LITTLE BOXES SCHOOL DISTRICTS FOSTER SEGREGATION;
BIG BOX SCHOOL DISTRICTS FACILITATE INTEGRATION

Metro area	Percentage of metro area students enrolled in city schools	Number of suburban school districts in 1999–2000	School segregation index	
			Blacks 1999–2000	Poor 1999–2000
Houston, Tex.	28%	42	70	55
Detroit, Mich.	25	102	89	64
Columbus, Ohio	27	50	70	52
Cleveland, Ohio	23	84	81	62
Nashville, Tenn.	34	8	56	na
Louisville, Ky.	61	12	45	40
Indianapolis, Ind.	17	52	67	46
Milwaukee, Wis.	48	37	78	64
Albuquerque, N. Mex.	73	6	36	50
Syracuse, N.Y.	18	35	74	42
Madison, Wis.	34	15	57	32
Harrisburg, Pa.	9	30	76	45
Raleigh, N.C.	41	6	38	35
Richmond, Va.	16	16	61	55

largest school district. In inelastic regions, the city school district, trapped within fixed boundaries, slowly shrank in enrollment and was surrounded by multiple suburban systems.

In elastic regions, the city school district might expand as the city annexes new property, but not always. Some city governments found that guaranteeing residents of to-be-annexed areas that their neighborhoods would remain part of their suburban school districts smoothed the path to annexation; Houston, Columbus, and Indianapolis all had city school districts much smaller than their expanding city limits. By contrast, Nashville, Albuquerque, and Raleigh were served by unified, county-wide districts.

Table 1.17 also measures school segregation metrowide by the same dissimilarity index used to measure residential segregation metrowide. With one exception, black students were much less segregated in elastic area schools than they were in inelastic area schools. The exception was Louisville, where, in 1975, a federal court ordered the merger of the Louisville and Jefferson County school districts.

Skeptics may argue that most southern school systems, like Louisville's, had federal court-ordered desegregation plans in effect. This was true, but because these systems were often countywide (Big Boxes), they typically linked city and suburb. Middle-class whites could not flee to little boxes school systems. Desegregation within such Big Box systems was more successful and more stable than in areas where school desegregation plans applied solely to an inner-city school system. Such limited school desegregation efforts often helped spur white flight to private schools or to suburban little boxes systems.

During the 1970s and 1980s, southern schools were much less segregated than southern neighborhoods. (Northern school enrollments generally mirrored housing patterns closely.) During the 1990s, however, an increasingly conservative federal judiciary, filled with over two decades of Republican appointees, accelerated the systematic dismantling of southern (and northern) desegregation orders. As a result, while residential segregation of African Americans diminished, segregation of their children increased in the public schools. Greater segregation of black pupils and Hispanic pupils (driven by major immigration) increased the level of economic school segregation during America's most sustained period of economic growth.

Lesson 22: Inelastic areas were harder hit by deindustrialization of the American labor market.

I would not argue that major economic changes are driven by urban development patterns. The deindustrialization of the American workforce, for example, was the result primarily of global competition and technological change in manufacturing in recent decades, not of the ways in which metro areas have developed.

Deindustrialization has affected urban areas very differently. Table 1.18 shows these effects during the last three decades (when deindustrialization had already begun from America's postwar industrial peak).

Inelastic cities reached maturity during the industrial age. In 1969 their metro areas were still more highly industrialized (28

TABLE 1.18
INELASTIC REGIONS WERE HARDER HIT BY
DEINDUSTRIALIZATION OF AMERICAN LABOR MARKET

Metro area	Manufacturing jobs as percentage of total jobs 1969	Change in number of manufacturing jobs 1969–1999	Change in number of manufacturing jobs 1989–1999	Manufacturing jobs as percentage of total jobs 1999
Houston, Tex.	16%	55%	28%	9%
Detroit, Mich.	34	−28	0	18
Columbus, Ohio	23	−18	1	9
Cleveland, Ohio	33	−38	−8	16
Nashville, Tenn.	21	36	11	12
Louisville, Ky.	30	−29	1	13
Indianapolis, Ind.	28	−22	1	12
Milwaukee, Wis.	33	−17	0	18
Albuquerque, N. Mex.	7	202	30	7
Syracuse, N.Y.	25	−30	−12	12
Madison, Wis.	12	86	21	9
Harrisburg, Pa.	22	−18	−12	11
Raleigh, N.C.	17	93	11	11
Richmond, Va.	19	−5	−6	9

percent) than were elastic metro areas (18 percent). Moreover, their industrial bases (particularly Detroit's, Cleveland's, and Milwaukee's) emphasized smokestack industries—steel, automobiles, and other metal trades. These industries were among those hardest hit by international competition. The loss of manufacturing jobs was catastrophic for Detroit, Cleveland, and Louisville.

Several elastic areas (Albuquerque, Madison, and Raleigh) grew up largely during the postindustrial era. New export products such as computers and electronic components often characterized these metro areas' industrial activities. Important also was manufacturing of nondurable products (like bread, dairy products, and printing) that served a growing regional population. Albuquerque, Madison, and Raleigh built impressively on small manufacturing bases. Yet manufacturing declined in importance in each of these elastic areas.

It is instructive to examine metro areas within the same region or state. This minimizes Sun Belt-Frost Belt confusion. For example, while inelastic Louisville lost industrial jobs (−29 percent), elastic Nashville gained (+36 percent); while inelastic Richmond lost industrial jobs (−5 percent), elastic Raleigh gained (+93 percent).

More striking are the contrasts between areas that have both been caught up by deindustrialization. Both Columbus and Cleveland lost many manufacturing jobs, but elastic Columbus (both a state capital and a college town) boomed while inelastic Cleveland stagnated. The percentage decline in manufacturing jobs was less in inelastic Milwaukee than in elastic Indianapolis, but Indianapolis was clearly the more economically vigorous area.

Lesson 23: Elastic areas had faster rates of nonfactory job creation than inelastic areas.

Whatever the trends in manufacturing, elastic areas had much greater rates of nonfactory job creation than inelastic areas (Table 1.19). Over the past three decades, all the elastic regions doubled or even tripled their nonfactory job supply. Inelastic areas also experienced net nonfactory job growth. Despite the impressive comeback of the industrial heartland in the 1990s, the rate of nonfactory job creation of elastic regions substantially out-

TABLE 1.19
ELASTIC AREAS HAD FASTER RATES OF
NONFACTORY JOB CREATION THAN INELASTIC AREAS

	Total nonmanufacturing job growth 1969–1999	Total nonmanufacturing job growth 1989–1999
Houston, Tex.	213%	34%
Detroit, Mich.	68	17
Columbus, Ohio	145	30
Cleveland, Ohio	53	17
Nashville, Tenn.	178	42
Louisville, Ky.	98	28
Indianapolis, Ind.	115	29
Milwaukee, Wis.	87	19
Albuquerque, N. Mex.	199	31
Syracuse, N.Y.	63	7
Madison, Wis.	135	31
Harrisburg, Pa.	96	19
Raleigh, N.C.	227	49
Richmond, Va.	114	19

stripped the rate of nonfactory job creation of inelastic regions during the last decade as well.

Lesson 24: Elastic areas showed greater real income gains than inelastic areas.

Job growth can be just a proxy for population growth. Did the standard of living of elastic area residents get better compared with that of inelastic area residents? The answer was yes, although not as dramatically as the differential in employment growth. From 1969 to 1999, real per capita personal income in these elastic areas as a group grew 115 percent compared with an average of 94 percent in inelastic areas (Table 1.20). During the booming 1990s, elastic regions maintained their edge in

TABLE 1.20
ELASTIC AREAS SHOWED GREATER REAL INCOME
GAINS THAN INELASTIC AREAS

	Percentage growth in real per capita personal income 1969–1999	Percentage growth in real per capita personal income 1989–1999
Houston, Tex.	119%	26%
Detroit, Mich.	83	14
Columbus, Ohio	103	18
Cleveland, Ohio	81	12
Nashville, Tenn.	132	23
Louisville, Ky.	106	21
Indianapolis, Ind.	98	19
Milwaukee, Wis.	94	19
Albuquerque, N. Mex.	117	18
Syracuse, N.Y.	77	5
Madison, Wis.	89	19
Harrisburg, Pa.	103	11
Raleigh, N.C.	147	19
Richmond, Va.	115	8

growth of real income (20 percent) over inelastic regions (13 percent).

Lesson 25: Elastic cities have better bond ratings than inelastic cities.

What were the fiscal consequences of these demographic, social, and economic patterns? Bond rating agencies must assess the risk associated with a city government's debts. Ratings are based on long-term economic outlook and past debt management. The highest rating (Aaa) indicates a blue-chip investment. A rating of Ba or lower indicates a junk bond, which typically cannot be purchased by pension funds and other institutional investors.

The debt management of some inelastic cities (for example, Milwaukee) was better than their social management (Table 1.21), but the pattern of the superiority of elastic cities over inelastic cities held. Elastic cities averaged Aa1 ratings. Inelastic cities averaged Al ratings—a full ratings point lower that meant hundreds of millions of dollars in higher interest rates paid.

Lesson 26: Elastic areas have a higher educated workforce than inelastic areas.

Past prosperity may have lulled old industrial areas into complacency. Many failed to tool up for economic change. Also, in the Old Economy, workers moved to jobs. In the New Economy, highly educated, creative people increasingly choose where they want to live based on regional lifestyle, and then jobs tend to move to where the creative people are located.

The workforce's education level was a good measure of adaptability of areas to the postindustrial, Information Age. A key measure of workforce quality is the percentage of highly edu-

TABLE 1.21
ELASTIC CITIES HAVE BETTER BOND
RATINGS THAN INELASTIC CITIES

Central city	City bond rating 2000
Houston, Tex.	Aaa
Detroit, Mich.	Baa3
Columbus, Ohio	Aaa
Cleveland, Ohio	A1
Nashville, Tenn.	Aa2
Louisville, Ky.	Aa3
Indianapolis, Ind.	Aaa
Milwaukee, Wis.	Aa2
Albuquerque, N. Mex.	Aa3
Syracuse, N.Y.	Baa1
Madison, Wis.	Aaa
Harrisburg, Pa.	Baa2
Raleigh, N.C.	Aaa
Richmond, Va.	Aa3

TABLE 1.22
ELASTIC AREAS HAVE A HIGHER EDUCATED
WORKFORCE THAN INELASTIC AREAS

	Percentage of area workers with bachelor's degree 2000	Percentage of area workers with graduate or professional degree 2000
Houston, Tex.	18.2%	9.0%
Detroit, Mich.	14.3	8.5
Columbus, Ohio	19.5	9.6
Cleveland, Ohio	14.9	8.4
Nashville, Tenn.	18.2	8.6
Louisville, Ky.	14.8	9.2
Indianapolis, Ind.	17.1	8.7
Milwaukee, Wis.	18.3	8.7
Albuquerque, N. Mex.	16.5	11.9
Syracuse, N.Y.	14.2	9.9
Madison, Wis.	24.8	15.8
Harrisburg, Pa.	14.4	8.2
Raleigh, N.C.	24.6	14.3
Richmond, Va.	19.5	9.8

cated workers. Table 1.22 shows that elastic regions consistently had higher proportions of college-educated workers than inelastic regions. The gap was particularly notable for Albuquerque, Madison, and Raleigh-Durham—locations both of major universities and of concentrations of high-tech industries—that had double-digit proportions of workers with graduate and professional degrees.

Having a highly educated labor force was both consequence and cause of having a high-tech economy. Indeed, the presence of a major, high-quality university was often an engine supporting local postindustrial growth. Between our two sample groups the major universities in elastic areas were Houston-Rice, Ohio State, Vanderbilt, Indiana-Purdue (Indianapolis campus), New Mexico, Wisconsin, and the Research Triangle's Duke-North Carolina-North Carolina State. Major universities in inelastic areas were Wayne State, Cleveland State-Case Western Reserve,

Louisville, Marquette-Wisconsin (Milwaukee campus), Syracuse, Dickinson College, and Virginia Commonwealth-Richmond.

With their more highly skilled labor forces and healthier central cities as living environments, elastic areas are better positioned for future economic growth in the information age.

Conclusion

Looking back over all the lessons, what composite profile can be drawn for inelastic and elastic areas?

An inelastic area has a central city frozen within its city limits and surrounded by growing suburbs. It may have a strong downtown business district as a regional employment center, but most city neighborhoods are increasingly catch basins for poor blacks and Hispanics. With the flight of middle-class families, the city's population has dropped steadily (typically by 20 percent or more). The income gap between city residents and suburbanites is wide, and typically widening. City government is squeezed between rising service needs and eroding incomes. Unable to tap the areas of greater economic growth (its suburbs), the city becomes increasingly reliant on federal and state aid. The suburbs are typically fragmented into multiple towns and small cities and mini school systems. This very fragmentation of local government reinforces racial and economic segregation. Rivalry among jurisdictions often inhibits the whole area's ability to respond to economic challenges.

In an elastic area suburban subdivisions expand around the central city, but the central city is able to expand as well and capture much of that suburban growth within its municipal boundaries. Although no community is free of racial inequities, minorities are more evenly spread throughout the area. Segregation by race and income class is reduced. City incomes are typically closer to (or sometimes higher) than suburban incomes. Tapping a broader tax base, an elastic city government is better financed and more inclined to rely on local resources to address local problems. In fact, local public institutions, in general, tend to be more unified and promote more united and effective responses to economic challenges.

Did the 1990s change this picture? Major Hispanic immigration slowed (or even reversed) some inelastic cities' population decline. The move back of young professionals and empty nesters to some regentrifying city neighborhoods, coupled with the steady movement of lower-income families to some older, inner suburbs, slowed down (or even slightly reversed) the city-suburb income gap. Inelastic cities were no longer plummeting in the 1990s, but the racial and economic chasms between inelastic cities and their suburbs remained profound. Elastic cities (and their regions) remained much better positioned for future progress.

Notes

1. The 1950 census did not identify Hispanics as either a racial or an ethnic group (aside from about 600,000 foreign-born Hispanics of Mexican and other Latin American origin). I have adopted an estimate of about 4 million Hispanics in 1950.

2. In 2000 a majority of all blacks lived in metropolitan New York, Chicago, Washington, D.C., Atlanta, Philadelphia, Detroit, Los Angeles, Houston, Baltimore, Dallas, New Orleans, Memphis, Norfolk-Virginia Beach-Newport News, St. Louis, Newark, Miami, Cleveland, Fort Lauderdale, Oakland, Charlotte, Richmond, Birmingham, Raleigh-Durham, Riverside-San Bernardino, Greensboro-Winston Salem, Tampa, and Boston. Adding Orange County, California, to these metro areas accounted for a majority of all Asians. Adding Phoenix and San Antonio covered a majority of all Hispanics.

3. The nine urbanized areas where density increased were four located in California (Los Angeles-Long Beach, San Diego, San Jose, and Riverside-San Bernardino), Miami-Hialeah, Florida, two Connecticut suburbs of New York City (Stamford and Norwalk), and two polar opposites (Atlantic City and Salt Lake City).

4. In 1950, twenty future central cities were either too small (e.g., Jonesboro and Rogers, Arkansas, or Myrtle Beach, South Carolina) for the census to report municipal area or they did not yet exist (e.g., Paradise, Lancaster, Irvine, Palm Desert, and Temecula, California, or Cape Coral and Port Saint Lucie, Florida).

5. Because of redefinition of some metro areas between 1990 and 2000 and more rapid growth of more elastic metro areas, the degree of variation among these pairs has increased somewhat since their original selection for *Cities without Suburbs*.

6. The designation of "elastic" or "inelastic" is always based on the characteristics of a central city. Although a metro area also will be referred to as an elastic area or inelastic area, that qualifier reflects its central city's status.

7. East Lansing (Michigan State), Evanston (Northwestern), New Brunswick (Rutgers), and West Lafayette (Purdue) also grew above 5,000 persons per square mile but had lost their designation as central cities by 2000.

8. Syracuse's having a capture/contribute percentage of –165 percent in the 1990s may require some explanation. Of all 14 regions, metro Syracuse was the

only one that actually lost population in the 1990s. The statistic means that the city's population loss (16,554) was 65 percent more than the metro area's total population loss (10,060) for the decade.

9. National Association of Home Builders, *Smart Growth: Building Better Places to Live, Work, and Play* (Washington, D.C., 2000), 8.

Chapter II

Characteristics of Metropolitan Areas

How does this concept of city elasticity affect demographic, social, and economic patterns of all cities and metro areas beyond the fourteen examined in chapter I? To analyze this phenomenon I have constructed an elasticity score for 521 central cities in the nation's 331 Metropolitan Statistical Areas.[1]

The 331 metro areas range in population from Los Angeles (9,519,338) to Enid, Oklahoma (57,813), in 2000. Lumping areas of such disparate size into common categories produces averages that hide more than they reveal. Therefore, I will exclude from further discussion the lowest end of the scale—the 149 metro areas with fewer than 250,000 residents in 2000.[2]

Of the 182 remaining metro areas, three other groups seem to march to a different drummer. For the following reasons these also are being excluded from my proposed categories.

First, I exclude three Mexican border towns: El Paso, McAllen-Edinburg-Mission, and Brownsville-Harlingen. Along with Laredo, a smaller metro area, these Texas communities sit on the northern bank of the Rio Grande opposite major Mexican communities. With high resident populations of Hispanics (78 percent to 94 percent) and thousands of Mexican workers and shoppers commuting daily across the border, these Texas cities are really economic and sociological extensions of northern Mexico.

Second, I exclude from further analysis seven White-only metro areas. These seven areas (Salt Lake City and Provo, Utah; Spokane, Washington; Eugene, Oregon; Boise, Idaho; Fort Collins, Colorado; and Springfield, Missouri) have few blacks (1.3 percent) and few Hispanics (6.3 percent). Their small black and Hispanic communities seem to be exposed only to minimal-to-moderate levels of residential and school segregation. Once again, including these areas in the larger analysis would distort the averages of the categories.[3]

The last group—city-less metro areas—is set apart for a purely technical reason. This group is composed of the four larger metro areas that the federal government has designated without central cities within their boundaries. Three are subunits of a Consolidated Metropolitan Statistical Area (CMSA). They are Long Island, New York (Nassau-Suffolk counties), and Bergen-Passaic and Middlesex-Somerset-Hunterdon counties in New Jersey. Within these areas, employment locations are highly dispersed; their real central city, of course, is New York City. The fourth city-less metro area is Honolulu, Hawaii. Since 1907 the island of Oahu (Honolulu County) has been governed by a consolidated government. The "city" of Honolulu is only a Census Designated Place and has never had a separate corporate existence whose growth I can track.

After excluding all of the above, I have 168 metro areas for further categorization. To cut down the variation further, I have separated out 49 large metro areas with principal central cities under 100,000 residents from those metro areas with principal central cities over 100,000 residents.

Among the 119 remaining major metro areas with principal central cities above 100,000 residents, the range of characteristics is still wide. Therefore, readers should not place too much emphasis on composite characteristics of different categories. The most telling tests of my point of view—the effects of urban elasticity and inelasticity—are comparisons of cities within the same region, state, or even metro area.

The results are summarized in Table 2.1. The elasticity score represents the combined effect of a city's density (population per square mile) in 1950 and the degree to which it expanded its city limits between 1950 and 2000. Each city's initial density and degree of boundary expansion (by percentage and absolute area) are ranked against those of all other cities in its group. A city's relative rankings (grouped into deciles) for the two key characteristics (initial density and boundary expansion) are added together to produce a composite elasticity score with the degree of boundary expansion awarded three times the weight of initial density.[4]

New York City ranks in the lowest decile (1) for having the highest population density in 1950 (25,046 per square mile). It also ranks in the lowest decile (1) for not expanding its city limits at all. Therefore, New York City's elasticity score is the minimum 4 [1 + (3 × 1)]. Anchorage, Alaska, ranks in the highest

TABLE 2.1
SUMMARY OF CATEGORIES

Category	Large metro areas	Small metro areas	Total metro areas
Mexican border towns	3	1	4
White-only metro areas	7	7	14
City-less metro areas	4	1	5
Large central cities (100,000+ residents)	119	0	119
Smaller central cities (fewer than 100,000 residents	49	0	49
Smallest central cities and metro areas	0	140	140
TOTAL	182	149	331

decile (10) for having among the lowest population densities in 1950 (900 per square mile). It ranks in the highest decile (10) for having one of the highest boundary expansion rates (13,482 percent). Therefore, Anchorage's elasticity score is the maximum 40 [10 + (3 × 10)].

I have ranked all cities by their elasticity scores and split them into five groupings: zero elasticity, low elasticity, medium elasticity, high elasticity, and hyper elasticity. (New York City is at the bottom of the zero-elasticity group; Anchorage leads the hyper-elasticity group.) The 119 largest areas are ranked in ascending order of elasticity (Table 2.2).

The 24-member zero-elasticity group includes three inelastic cities analyzed in chapter I (Detroit, Cleveland, and Syracuse). This group also includes New York, Philadelphia, Baltimore, St. Louis, Buffalo, Newark, and Washington, D.C.—often found on lists of troubled cities. In addition, the zero-elasticity group includes Boston, San Francisco, and Minneapolis—cities seen as being in relatively good shape.

The 23-member low-elasticity group includes Milwaukee, Louisville, and Richmond (discussed in chapter 1) as well as Los Angeles, Chicago, Seattle, Denver, New Orleans, Cincinnati, Oakland, and Norfolk. It may be surprising to find Chicago edging (just barely) into the low-elasticity group. However, in the

---

Box 2.1 Whatever Happened to the City of Spring Garden?

What ever happened to the cities of Spring Garden, Northern Liberties, Kensington, Southwark, and Moyamensing? In 1850 these Pennsylvania communities were the ninth, eleventh, twelfth, twentieth, and twenty-eighth most populous cities in America. Four years later they were consolidated with the larger city of Philadelphia and unincorporated areas of Philadelphia County to create the boundaries of the city of Philadelphia as we know it today.

In fact, ten of the country's fifty largest cities in 1850 disappeared before 1900. All were consolidated into larger governmental bodies.

In 1867 Boston annexed the city of Roxbury; seven years later it leaped across Boston Harbor to annex the city of Charlestown. Allegheny in 1907 was taken in by Pittsburgh. And in the tradition of little fish-big fish-bigger fish, the twenty-fourth largest city in 1850, Williamsburg, was annexed in 1854 by the city of Brooklyn (seventh largest), which in turn became part of New York City in 1898 (Box 1.2).

The political geography of mature metropolitan areas may appear immutable to their residents today, but a century ago compelling public interests were served by such consolidations. Popular opposition as well as natural obstacles (harbors and rivers) had to be overcome, but the effort was worthwhile. These new governmental structures served their communities well for many decades.

1950s Chicago annexed 17 square miles west of the city where O'Hare International Airport and vast office and warehouse complexes are located.

Of the cities analyzed in chapter I, Columbus and Madison are among the 25 medium-elasticity cities as well as Portland (Oregon), Atlanta, and Sacramento.

Indianapolis-Marion and Raleigh are among the 23 high-elasticity cities as well as Dallas, Memphis, and Kansas City (Missouri).

Finally, the 24 hyper-elasticity cities include Houston, Nashville-Davidson, and Albuquerque (analyzed in chapter I), along with all other major city-county consolidations (Jacksonville-Duval, Lexington-Fayette, Columbus-Muskogee, Au-

TABLE 2.2

119 MAJOR METRO AREAS GROUPED BY PRINCIPAL CENTRAL CITY'S ELASTICITY

Zero elasticity	Elasticity score	Low elasticity	Elasticity score	Medium elasticity	Elasticity score	High Elasticity	Elasticity score	Hyper elasticity	Elasticity score
NEW YORK, NY	4.0	CHICAGO, IL	11.5	PEORIA, IL	19.5	KNOXVILLE, TN	26.5	LITTLE ROCK, AR	31.0
NEWARK, NJ	4.0	OAKLAND, CA	11.5	ANN ARBOR*, MI	19.5	MODESTO*, CA	26.5	ALBUQUERQUE, NM	31.0
BOSTON, MA	4.0	ALLENTOWN, PA	11.5	DES MOINES, IA	19.5	SANTA ROSA*, CA	26.5	LAS VEGAS*, NV	31.0
DETROIT, MI	4.0	CINCINNATI, OH	11.5	ROCKFORD, IL	20.5	SHREVEPORT, LA	27.0	HUNTSVILLE*, AL	31.0
WASHINGTON, DC	4.0	ERIE, PA	13.0	FORT LAUDERDALE*, FL	20.5	LAFAYETTE*, LA	27.0	SAN DIEGO, CA	31.5
HARTFORD, CT	5.0	SEATTLE, WA	13.0	SALINAS*, CA	20.5	WICHITA, KS	27.5	LEXINGTON, KY	32.0
ROCHESTER, NY	5.0	STAMFORD, CT	13.0	VENTURA*, CA	21.0	TAMPA, FL	28.0	SAN ANTONIO, TX	32.0
ST LOUIS, MO	5.5	NEW ORLEANS, LA	13.5	PORTLAND, OR	21.5	MOBILE, AL	28.5	MONTGOMERY, AL	32.0
PROVIDENCE, RI	5.5	LOUISVILLE, KY	14.0	ANAHEIM*, CA	22.0	JACKSON, MS	28.5	HOUSTON, TX	32.0
SYRACUSE, NY	6.0	GRAND RAPIDS, MI	15.0	SAVANNAH, GA	22.5	FRESNO, CA	28.5	COLUMBUS, GA	32.5
MINNEAPOLIS, MN	6.5	FLINT, MI	15.0	ATLANTA, GA	23.0	MEMPHIS, TN	29.0	NASHVILLE, TN	33.0
SAN FRANCISCO, CA	7.0	AKRON, OH	15.0	DENVER, CO	23.0	TULSA, OK	29.0	AUGUSTA, GA	33.0
BUFFALO, NY	7.0	TACOMA, WA	15.0	OMAHA, NE	23.0	COLUMBIA, SC	29.5	SAN JOSE, CA	33.0
PITTSBURGH, PA	8.0	LOS ANGELES, CA	15.5	FORT WAYNE, IN	23.5	CHATTANOOGA, TN	29.5	CORPUS CHRISTI, TX	33.0
CLEVELAND, OH	8.0	MILWAUKEE, WI	16.0	VALLEJO*, CA	23.5	RENO*, NV	29.5	JACKSONVILLE, FL	34.0
BALTIMORE, MD	8.0	TOLEDO, OH	16.5	RIVERSIDE*, CA	24.5	INDIANAPOLIS, IN	29.5	BAKERSFIELD*, CA	34.0
NEW HAVEN, CT	8.0	NORFOLK, VA	16.5	MADISON, WI	24.5	KANSAS CITY, MO	30.0	CHARLOTTE, NC	34.0
JERSEY CITY NJ	8.5	DAYTON, OH	17.0	STOCKTON, CA	24.5	FAYETTEVILLE*, NC	30.0	PHOENIX, AZ	35.0
PHILADELPHIA, PA	8.5	RICHMOND, VA	17.0	BATON ROUGE, LA	25.0	FORT WORTH, TX	30.0	TALLAHASSEE*, FL	35.0
LOWELL, MA	9.0	SOUTH BEND, IN	17.0	BIRMINGHAM, AL	25.0	RALEIGH, NC	30.0	AUSTIN, TX	35.0
WORCESTER, MA	9.0	EVANSVILLE, IN	17.5	SACRAMENTO, CA	25.5	GREENSBORO, NC	30.0	COLORADO SPRINGS, CO	35.5
SPRINGFIELD, MA	9.0	GARY*, IN	18.0	SALEM*, OR	25.5	DALLAS, TX	30.5	TUCSON*, AZ	35.5
BRIDGEPORT, CT	9.5	LANSING, MI	18.5	BEAUMONT, TX	26.0	ORLANDO, FL	30.5	OKLAHOMA CITY, OK	37.0
MIAMI, FL	10.0			COLUMBUS, OH	26.0			ANCHORAGE*, AK	40.0
				LINCOLN, NE	26.0				

An asterisk (*) indicates that the city was not identified as a central city in the 1950 census.

Box 2.2 *Poverty and Place* Tracks Black Ghetto Expansion

The definitive study of trends in concentrated poverty is *Poverty and Place: Ghettos, Barrios, and the American City* by Paul A. Jargowsky (Russell Sage Foundation, 1997). In his study of 318 metro areas between 1980 and 1990, Jargowsky, a University of Texas at Dallas social scientist, found that black ghetto poverty increased significantly.

Defining a black ghetto as an urban census tract in which 40 percent or more of the black population is poor, Jargowsky found that the number of blacks living in ghetto areas increased 36 percent from 4.3 million to 5.9 million.

The percentage of the total black population living in ghetto areas increased from 20 percent to almost 24 percent—which, however, meant that over three-quarters of the black population did not live in urban ghettos. Poor blacks, however, were increasingly isolated from the black middle class. The proportion of poor urban blacks in ghetto areas increased from 37 percent to 45 percent.

Most ominous for many city officials, the physical size of urban ghettos expanded dramatically during the 1980s even as, with the flight of the black middle class to suburbs, the population density of ghettos declined. The number of census tracts classified as ghettos grew from 3,256 to 5,003—a 54 percent increase!—while population density declined –11 percent in ghetto areas.

"From the point of view of local political officials, the increase in the size of the ghetto is a disaster," Jargowsky comments. "Many of those leaving the ghetto settle in non-ghetto areas outside the political jurisdiction of the central city. Thus, the geo-

---

gusta-Richmond, and Anchorage-Anchorage Borough). The list of hyper-elasticity cities is rounded out by such annexation powerhouses as San Diego, San Antonio, Phoenix, San Jose, Austin, Charlotte, Oklahoma City, and Tucson.

A similar analysis has been applied to the 49 metro areas with principal central cities under 100,000 (Harrisburg is a zero-elasticity member of this category) as well as to the 149 smaller metro areas. (All 521 central cities are categorized by their relative elasticity in Appendix A.)

Table 2.3 summarizes the average population growth of the metro areas in each group. The zero-elasticity group began and ended with the largest average metro population and experi-

graphic size of the ghetto is expanding, cutting a wider swath through the hearts of our metropolitan areas."

Jargowsky found that ghetto poverty was a function of both racial segregation and metropolitan economic growth. During the 1980s, the proportion of blacks living in ghettos increased most dramatically in the declining industrial states and oil patch communities caught in the oil and real estate slump. By contrast, booming, postindustrial economies around Boston, Hartford, New York, Philadelphia, Baltimore, and Washington allowed many middle-class blacks to leave ghettos for new suburban homes.

"Ghetto poverty," Jargowsky concluded, "is not primarily the product of a 'ghetto culture' that discourages upward mobility, but the product of metropolitan labor markets and residential settlement patterns. Ghetto self-help programs, enterprise zones, etc., cannot alter the fundamental dynamics of metropolitan economies or the evolving geography of residential location decisions.

"Vigorous enforcement of antidiscrimination in housing, scattered-site public housing, and zoning requirements that encourage mixed-income developments can all play a role in reducing the segregation of blacks and the black poor," Jargowsky recommends. "This has both an immediate effect—reducing ghetto poverty—and a direct, long-term effect—the increased earnings potential of children who attend better schools, grow up in safer, more stimulating environments, and see better role models of success in the mainstream economy."

Despite the economic boom of the 1990s, there is little evidence these patterns changed significantly.

enced the lowest rate of metro population growth (47 percent). The other groups doubled, tripled, or even quadrupled their average populations.[5] Disparities in growth rates, however important, should not be allowed to obscure the fact that all groups, including the zero-elasticity group, added an average of 650,000 to 850,000 residents between 1950 and 2000.

What about the factors that affected different central cities' elasticity? Table 2.4 illustrates the average population density in 1950 of central cities in each group. At 12,757 persons per square mile (or 226 percent of the average for 521 central cities of 5,657 persons per square mile), the zero-elasticity cities had little vacant land for new, low-density subdivision development; they

TABLE 2.3
ALMOST ALL METRO AREAS HAVE GROWN

Metro area	Average metro population		Percentage change 1950–2000	Percentage change 1990s
	1950	2000		
Zero Elasticity	1,544,141	2,263,589	47%	7%
Low Elasticity	853,498	1,655,573	94	9
Medium Elasticity	322,242	1,098,720	241	22
High Elasticity	358,068	1,021,222	185	22
Hyper Elasticity	291,996	1,141,542	291	26

had little alternative but to try to expand their boundaries. The low-elasticity cities were also above the national average. Medium-, high-, and hyper-elasticity cities had some room to grow internally—although they would expand their boundaries dramatically as well.

Table 2.5 demonstrates that double-barreled advantage. The zero-elasticity cities barely expanded their city limits (statistically, by 1 percent); typically, they expanded through lakefront, riverfront, and bayshore reclamation (or, simply, from more accurate surveying). The low-elasticity cities expanded modestly (21 percent), but the medium-, high-, and hyper-elasticity cities spread far and wide across the landscape, expanding three-, four-, and tenfold in territory, respectively. (Setting aside An-

TABLE 2.4
LOW-DENSITY CITIES CAN GROW THROUGH
IN-FILL; HIGH-DENSITY CITIES CANNOT

Central city	Average city density (persons per square mile) 1950	Average city density as a percentage of national average city density 1950
Zero Elasticity	12,757	226%
Low Elasticity	6,879	122
Medium Elasticity	5,280	93
High Elasticity	4,822	85
Hyper Elasticity	4,729	84

TABLE 2.5
ELASTIC CITIES EXPAND THEIR CITY LIMITS;
INELASTIC CITIES DO NOT

	Average city area (square miles)		Percentage change	
Central cities	1950	2000	1950–2000	in 1990s
Zero Elasticity	57	58	1%	0%
Low Elasticity	69	84	21	0
Medium Elasticity	27	79	193	7
High Elasticity	33	146	342	7
Hyper Elasticity	33	345	944	11

chorage's massive, 1,686-square-mile land grab, hyper-elastic cities still expanded eightfold in land area.)

By 2000 the average zero-elasticity city was the smallest in geographic area (58 square miles), although the group covered a wide range in municipal size from Jersey City (15 square miles) to New York City (303 square miles). By contrast, the average hyper-elasticity city was six times as large geographically.

The demographic payoff is summed up in Table 2.6, which shows each group's relative capture/contribute percentage. Over the five decades zero-elasticity cities contributed –21 percent of their regions' new-home buyers; in other words, these central cities provided 21 percent of their own suburbs' population growth. Low-elasticity cities essentially broke even (3 per-

TABLE 2.6
ELASTIC CITIES CAPTURE SUBURBAN GROWTH;
INELASTIC CITIES CONTRIBUTE TO SUBURBAN GROWTH

Area/city	Average capture/ contribute percentage 1950–2000	Average capture/ contribute percentage in the 1990s
Zero Elasticity	–21%	8%
without New York City	–22	–11
Low Elasticity	3	7
Medium Elasticity	15	14
High Elasticity	26	19
Hyper Elasticity	50	43

cent). Medium-elasticity cities captured a modest 15 percent, and high-elasticity cities a somewhat higher 26 percent. Hyper-elasticity cities, however, captured half of their regions' net population growth. Moreover, these patterns continued in the 1990s. Zero-elasticity cities are the victims of their suburbs, but high- and hyper-elasticity cities often *are* their own suburbs.

Table 2.7 demonstrates the dramatically different consequences on the population trends among central cities. The 24 zero-elasticity cities lost population (an average of −20 percent) except for New York, Miami, San Francisco, and Lowell, Massachusetts. These four cities' recent population gains were fueled entirely by Asian and Hispanic immigration. If New York City is excluded, zero-elasticity cities' population loss was −33 percent.

Low-elasticity cities as a group gained five percent in population; that gain was largely the result of Los Angeles's being in this category. Most of these cities' annexation activities occurred in the 1950s and 1960s, and population began to fall thereafter. Seventeen of 23 low-elasticity cities lost population since their historic population peaks.

Among the 25 medium-elasticity cities (which gained 80 percent in population overall), only Peoria, Des Moines, Savannah, and Birmingham (four cities whose annexations slowed down in recent years) lost population since earlier peaks. Fueled by white gentrification, Atlanta (which had dropped −19 percent between 1960 and 1990) made a strong comeback in the 1990s.

TABLE 2.7
ELASTIC CITIES GAIN POPULATION;
INELASTIC CITIES LOSE POPULATION

City	Average central city population		Percentage Change	
	1950	2000	1950–2000	1990s
Zero Elasticity	893,524	713,917	−20%	2%
without New York City	589,244	396,771	−33	−4
Low Elasticity	480,702	506,387	5	2
without Los Angeles	412,990	361,458	−12	0
Medium Elasticity	143,100	256,995	80	12
High Elasticity	155,917	327,322	109	12
Hyper Elasticity	135,653	559,223	312	22

Among the 47 high- and hyper-elasticity cities, only Kansas City, Missouri, had a slightly smaller population in 2000 than in 1950. (Kansas City annexed massive territory northward leading to its international airport, but most new, middle-income subdivisions were built south of the city in Johnson County, Kansas.) High-elasticity cities doubled in population (109 percent), but hyper-elasticity cities quadrupled their number of residents (312 percent).

Of course, all such categorizations of elasticity are based on history. The fact that a central city may have annexed much of its region's new development in the past is no guarantee that it will continue to be elastic in the future. By 2000, however, absent major Hispanic immigration, the truth of Lesson 14 (see chapter I) has been demonstrated many times: when a city stops growing, it starts shrinking.

The social and economic consequences of these striking differences in city-suburb dynamics are illustrated in the next several tables. Table 2.8 shows that all groups had roughly the same percentage of black residents metrowide (from 12 percent to 18 percent) in 2000. The racial profile of central cities, however, differed substantially.

Because of the high concentration of blacks within the inner city, zero-elasticity cities were 34 percent black. On a neighborhood-by-neighborhood basis, the black segregation index was a very high 68 in zero-elasticity metro areas (that is, in little boxes regions).

TABLE 2.8

INELASTIC AREAS ARE MORE RACIALLY
SEGREGATED THAN ELASTIC AREAS

| Metro area | Average percentage black in 2000 | | | Average metro segregation index* 2000 | Average index improvement 1990s |
	Metro area	City	Suburbs		
Zero Elasticity	13%	34%	7%	68	−3
Low Elasticity	15	32	8	65	−4
Medium Elasticity	12	21	8	57	−6
High Elasticity	18	29	12	55	−5
Hyper Elasticity	15	20	11	49	−5

*Segregation index: scale 0 to 100 (100 = total apartheid); lower numbers represent improvement

By contrast, hyper-elasticity cities embraced so much of their own suburban development that the proportion of blacks in the city (20 percent) was not that much higher than the percentage metrowide (15 percent). On a metrowide basis, the index of black segregation in these Big Box regions was 49 (significantly lower but still unacceptable).

At the peak period of residential segregation around 1970, black segregation indices typically ranged in the 70s, 80s, and even low 90s. However, residential segregation of blacks has been steadily (if too slowly) reduced in most metro areas. In the 1990s, black segregation indices fell by one or more points in 105 of the 119 metro areas with the biggest reductions occurring in Portland (–18 points) and Salem (–16 points). (Both communities, I would observe, are located in Oregon with its strong, antisprawl, land use and housing laws.) In the other 14 metro areas, black segregation indices varied by less than a point from 1990 levels. In 2000, the most segregated metro area was Detroit (85); the most integrated metro area was Albuquerque (31).

As suggested in chapter I, segregation of Hispanics was primarily influenced by immigration patterns. This is illustrated by Table 2.9 that departs from my analysis of the impact of relative elasticity. Table 2.9 divides the 119 metro areas into groups of five according to the average increase in the Hispanic percentage of the regional population in the 1990s. The group with the

TABLE 2.9
MAJOR IMMIGRATION INCREASES HISPANIC SEGREGATION

Metro area	Average change in percentage points in Hispanic percentage of population 1990–2000	Average change in Hispanic segregation index 1990–2000	Average metro population in 2000	Average Hispanic percentage of metro population in 2000	Average Hispanic segregation index* in 2000
1st quintile	8.5	3.4	2,252,328	29%	48
2nd quintile	4.3	3.0	1,784,550	16	50
3rd quintile	2.7	2.3	1,095,378	9	48
4th quintile	1.4	–2.4	953,033	3	42
5th quintile	0.6	–9.4	913,026	2	32

*Segregation index: scale 0 to 100 (100 = total apartheid); lower numbers represent improvement

highest average increase in Hispanic population (8.5 percentage points) had the highest average increase in the Hispanic segregation index (3.4 percentage points). At the other end of the scale, the group with the lowest increase in Hispanic population (0.6 percentage points) actually experienced a substantial decrease in the Hispanic segregation index (–9.4 percentage points). As the succeeding columns show, average metro population size and proportion of Hispanic population vaguely influenced the overall level of Hispanic segregation. It was the dynamics of immigration, however, that largely determined whether or not Hispanic segregation increased or decreased.

The analysis of economic disparities returns to the relative elasticity format in Table 2.10. Highly racially segregated regions are highly economically segregated regions. Contrary to the trends for black segregation, between 1970 and 1990 economic segregation increased in 57 of 86 metro areas for which data were available; economic segregation was stable in eight metro areas and declined in 21 metro areas (all located in the Sun Belt). Jim Crow by income, however, is replacing Jim Crow by race. By 1999, the height of the economic boom, the pattern reversed modestly.

Table 2.11 analyzes patterns in income among the elasticity groups. Fifty years ago, median family incomes in central cities equaled or exceeded median family incomes for entire regions. There was a rough parity between city and suburban incomes. Thereafter, in the Age of Sprawl, central city incomes dropped below metrowide medians. For zero-elasticity cities, the decline

TABLE 2.10
HIGHLY RACIALLY SEGREGATED REGIONS ARE
HIGHLY ECONOMICALLY SEGREGATED REGIONS

Metro area (no.)	Average metro economic segregation index			
	1970	1980	1990	2000
Zero Elasticity (21)	35	39	42	40
Low Elasticity (19)	33	36	39	39
Medium Elasticity (14)	31	31	34	35
High Elasticity (16)	34	34	34	34
Hyper Elasticity (16)	35	32	34	34

*Segregation index: scale 0 to 100 (100 = total apartheid); lower numbers represent improvement

TABLE 2.11
INELASTIC CITIES HAVE WIDE INCOME GAPS WITH SUBURBS;
ELASTIC CITIES MAINTAIN GREATER CITY-SUBURB BALANCE

Central city	City percentage of metro median family income		City percentage of suburban per capita income	
	1950	2000	1990	2000
Zero Elasticity	95%	75%	70%	68%
Low Elasticity	101	83	79	78
Medium Elasticity	106	93	91	89
High Elasticity	109	98	100	97
Hyper Elasticity	106	100	104	102

was precipitous; they plummeted 29 percentage points to only 66 percent of the regionwide median by 2000. For hyper-elasticity cities that incorporated so many of their suburbs within their expanding city limits, the relative decline was much less; they slid only nine percentage points to 97 percent of the regionwide median family income in 2000.

The growing economic imbalance between cities and suburbs is made clearer by contrasting per capita income levels in central cities with suburban per capita income levels. By 1990, zero-elasticity cities' per capita incomes had fallen to only 70 percent of suburban levels. Despite the media-touted comeback of many older central cities and Census 2000's recording incomes for 1999, the peak year of the economic boom, the city-to-suburb income gap for all categories of cities widened slightly in the 1990s. Zero-elasticity cities dropped slightly to 68 percent in 2000. By contrast, hyper-elasticity cities had maintained income parity with their suburbs up to 1990 (104 percent) and largely held that position of parity in 2000 (102 percent).

Another critical measure of the economic health of central cities is the fair share of poverty index (Table 2.12). In 2000, poverty was much more concentrated in inelastic cities than in elastic cities. Inelastic cities were cast in the role of home for most of their metro areas' poor minorities, as clearly indicated by disparities in the central cities' fair share of poverty index. In 1990, zero-elasticity cities had almost twice the fair share of poverty (an index of 216) than hyper-elasticity cities had (115). In 2000, despite a decade of prosperity, those relationships were unchanged.

TABLE 2.12
POVERTY IS MORE DISPROPORTIONATELY CONCENTRATED
IN INELASTIC CITIES THAN IN ELASTIC CITIES

Metro area	Poverty rate in 2000		City fair share of poverty index 2000	City fair share of poverty index 1990
	Metro	City		
Zero Elasticity	10.9%	22.9%	220	216
Low Elasticity	10.8	19.2	180	174
Medium Elasticity	11.1	16.4	149	141
High Elasticity	12.8	16.8	134	133
Hyper Elasticity	12.9	14.8	115	115

Moreover, elastic cities' lesser concentration of poverty by jurisdiction was not just an artifact of these cities being larger proportions of their metro areas. As Table 2.10 shows, elastic regions also had somewhat less concentration of poverty on a neighborhood by neighborhood basis. Controlling planning, zoning, and housing policy for a larger portion of the region, elastic cities have the capacity to help spread low- and moderate-income housing across a wide range of neighborhoods.

In chapter I, I presented several explanations for these disparities in racial and income distribution. I will now review them in the context of this broader analysis.

First, differences in racial and economic segregation are not related to the proportion of blacks or poor people in an area. (As illustrated in Table 2.9, metro population size and the proportion of Hispanics do have a weak relationship with the level of Hispanic segregation.) Areas with high proportions of blacks or poor individuals may be highly segregated or quite well integrated. Similarly, areas with low proportions of blacks and poor persons may find them well blended into the larger community or highly isolated.

Second, although the proportion of minorities metrowide seems to have little to do with the degree of racial segregation, the historic distribution, or racial profile, plays some role. Traditionally, blacks and Hispanics have lived in rural and small-town areas in the South and West but not in the Northeast and Midwest. As urbanization has reached into the countryside, southern and western cities have not encountered as sharp racial gradients as have northeastern and midwestern cities.

Third, the absolute size of the metro area has little effect on the racial and economic isolation of city dwellers. Some of the country's largest cities and metro areas are concentrated within the zero-elasticity category, which suggests that metro and city population size is a factor. However, the relationship of population size to segregation (racial and economic) is weak.

More significant is the maturity of the city. Table 2.13 depicts the average date by which cities in each group passed the 100,000 population mark. On average, the zero-elasticity cities passed the mark in 1885, and the low-elasticity cities passed the mark in 1913. Generally, these were pre-automobile age cities. On average, by contrast, medium-, high-, and hyper-elasticity cities reached 100,000 residents in 1947, 1949, and 1954, entering into the era of the dominance of the suburban lifestyle.

A central city's age has many implications. By definition, an old city has an inventory of old, often decaying neighborhoods that typically become home to many poor people. A long-established black or Hispanic population in an old city may have become highly isolated as victims of the social prejudices of an earlier era. Even an old city's long participation in certain social welfare programs, such as public housing, may reinforce racial and economic isolation. In any event, a city's age strongly influences racial and economic segregation within a metro area.

Finally, a central city's elasticity has the highest relationship of all these factors to the level of racial and economic segregation in a metro area. Why some central cities expanded and others did not must really be the subject of case-by-case studies. My five categories of elasticity bring together many different cities

TABLE 2.13
INELASTIC CITIES ARE OLDER THAN ELASTIC CITIES

	Census when the population exceeded 100,000
Zero Elasticity	1885
Low Elasticity	1913
Medium Elasticity	1947
High Elasticity	1949
Hyper Elasticity	1954

from many different regions, but some general observations can be made.

In general, state laws regarding annexation are less inhibiting in the South and West than they are in the Northeast and Midwest. Old cities (often in the Northeast and Midwest) had more neighbors to contend and compete with than had younger cities (often in the South and West). Lesser racial gradients in the South and West raised fewer social and political barriers to a city's outward expansion. And being the hub of a more rapidly growing metro area created a more expansionist outlook among local public officials than was true of political leadership within more slowly expanding areas.

Finally, the relative unity or fragmentation of local government and institutions influences racial and economic segregation. Table 2.14 summarizes the rough picture in terms of local units of general government. The percentage of the area's population that is governed by the central city is listed in the first column. In effect, this statistic tells what proportion of the metro community falls under a single planning and zoning authority.

What does it mean for a zero-elasticity or low-elasticity city to have planning and zoning authority over about one-quarter of the metro area population? It means little since that city is no longer planning for new growth that can capture a share of the middle-class, suburban-style population.

By contrast, it is significant when a hyper-elasticity city represents more than half of the area because that city is planning for and capturing more than half of the area's suburban-style

TABLE 2.14
LITTLE BOXES REGIONS FOSTER SEGREGATION;
BIG BOX REGIONS FACILITATE INTEGRATION

Metro area	Percentage of area population governed by central city	Metropolitan power diffusion index 1992	Segregation index	
			Blacks 2000	Poor 2000
Zero Elasticity	25%	7.52	68	40
Low Elasticity	28	5.30	65	39
Medium Elasticity	33	4.87	57	35
High Elasticity	36	4.10	55	34
Hyper Elasticity	54	3.59	49	34

growth. How an elastic city government shapes the mix and distribution of new housing, new shopping areas, and new business parks makes a big difference in the future racial and economic profile of the area.

The second column in Table 2.14 summarizes the results of the Metropolitan Power Diffusion Index (Box 2.3). Devised by David Miller of the University of Pittsburgh, the MPDI calculates the degree to which responsibility for seventeen public services is either centralized or diffused at the local government level. The higher the index number, the more governmental responsibilities are diffused or decentralized. With one dominant central city and only two other small municipalities, metro Albuquerque's MPDI was 2.03 in 1992. With 232 local governments, metro Detroit's MPDI was 9.09. Paralleling my concept of little boxes and Big Box regions, zero-elasticity regions have the greatest diffusion (an MPDI of 7.52 in 1992) and hyper-elasticity regions have the greatest concentration (3.59) of local governmental responsibility.

The fragmentation of planning and zoning authority among multiple suburban governments in zero-elasticity areas is serious because these suburban governments are planning for most of the area's new growth. Balkanization of the suburbs inevitably promotes exclusive planning and zoning. By contrast, suburban balkanization around more elastic cities is both less widespread and less significant because these independent, suburban governments are typically planning for less than half of the area's expansion.

Table 2.15 relates the relative unity or fragmentation of public education to racial segregation in public school systems metrowide. The same racial and economic patterns characterized elementary school enrollments as occurred in housing markets. With the city schools surrounded by a plethora of suburban, little boxes districts, schools in inelastic areas were notably more segregated than schools in more elastic, less fragmented Big Box regions. However, in the 1970s and 1980s, with large, often countywide school districts under federal desegregation orders, southern schools were more integrated than southern neighborhoods. During the 1990s, a more conservative federal judiciary steadily dismantled desegregation plans, sending black children back to neighborhood schools that were racially and economically segregated.

Do these differences in the degree of fragmentation of local government and local education help explain the differences in

Box 2.3 Little Boxes Split Society, Slow Economy

University of Pittsburgh's David Y. Miller has published a short, but definitive book on *The Regional Governing of Metropolitan America* (Westview Press, 2002). Based on rigorous statistical research of all metro areas, Miller reaches key findings about the impact of governmental fragmentation, which Miller labels "diffusion."

- "Even when accounting for population [size] and region [of the country], jurisdictional diffusion is significantly and unquestionably linked to Black segregation in metropolitan America."
- "At least historically, power devolved to the local governments within the state creates the necessary condition for greater economic performance. However, when local governments fail to unify that devolved authority at the metropolitan level, the opportunity is lost. . . . Centralized state systems and decentralized metropolitan region systems underperform, in economic development, empowered but more centralized metropolitan regions."
- "Too much diffusion of power in metropolitan areas serves to increase the probability of racial segregation and to deter the ability of the metropolitan region to take advantage of economic expansion occurring within the region."
- "Gaps between rich and poor communities will always be a part of the metropolitan environment. . . . However, the distance between rich and poor should be minimized or, at least, kept from widening. . . . In the Allegheny county case, the gap between the richer and poorer communities is growing – and at an alarming rate. . . . Indeed, competition feeds upon itself and makes the competitive more competitive and the non-competitive more non-competitive."

Of the larger regions targeted in my chapter II, Miller's Metropolitan Power Diffusion Index rated the ten most governmentally diffuse regions as Philadelphia, St. Louis, Boston, Chicago, Pittsburgh, Scranton-Wilkes Barre, Minneapolis-St. Paul, Detroit, Harrisburg, and Allentown-Bethlehem-Easton; the ten most centralized regions were Columbus (Georgia), Norfolk-Virginia Beach-Newport News, Lubbock, Albuquerque, Tucson, Lincoln, Little Rock, Reno, Las Vegas, and Richmond.

The Metropolitan Power Diffusion Index (see <http://www.gspia.pitt.edu/mpdi/>) is a powerful analytic tool for understanding why Big Box regions outperform little boxes regions.

TABLE 2.15
LITTLE BOXES SCHOOL DISTRICTS FOSTER SEGREGATION;
BIG BOX SCHOOL DISTRICTS FACILITATE INTEGRATION

Metro area	Percentage of metro area pupils enrolled in city schools	Metropolitan Power Diffusion index for schools	Elementary school segregation index	
			Blacks 1999–2000	Poor 1999–2000
Zero Elasticity	29%	6.12	73	56
Low Elasticity	31	4.65	67	50
Medium Elasticity	35	3.76	60	46
High Elasticity	41	3.12	57	43
Hyper Elasticity	45	3.15	51	45

racial and economic segregation among different metro areas? I believe they do, based on my analysis, the excellent scholarship of others (Box 2.3), and on personal experience as an elected public official.

It matters whether a mayor or school board member shaping local policy sees poor blacks, Hispanics, and Asians as "our people here" or "those people there." Too often suburban officials (and they are usually white) see "those people there," when they look at the declining, decaying, impoverished, minority-dominated inner city. Too often city officials (and they are increasingly black and Hispanic) see only what can be done immediately for "our people here" when confronted with the still overwhelmingly white outer city.

The unspoken mission of most little boxes town councils and little boxes school boards is "to keep our town (or our schools) just the way they are for people just like *us*"—whoever "us" happens to be (Box 2.4). In a more unified area, a Big Box mayor or school board member will often see all groups as common constituents, deserving to be served in a fair and equitable way.

What is the interaction between economic trends and these patterns of metro development? The relationship between a central city's economic health and its suburbs' economic health has provoked lively debate in recent years. Many suburbanites believe they are economically independent of the city. Certainly there are many examples of highly prosperous individual suburban communities outside the most depressed central cities, like Bloomfield Hills outside Detroit. And with the increasing migration of jobs to suburban office complexes and industrial parks, many argue that edge cities are the wave of the future or even that, in the Internet age, cities will become superfluous.

The bulk of evidence, however, supports the view that cities and suburbs are all in it together. All are part of a regional economy whose overall fortunes are shaped primarily by constant changes in technology, consumer tastes, competition (increasingly global), transportation and communications linkages, investment capital flows, labor force quality, and other economic forces. One very compelling new theory of economic development is that America has entered an age where much economic development is driven by where members of the creative class cluster (Box 2.5). People do not move to jobs; jobs move to where talented, highly creative people chose to live largely for quality of life considerations.

One dramatic economic trend in recent decades has been the deindustrialization of the American economy. In 1950, for example, the largest segment of the American workforce (33 percent) was engaged in manufacturing; by 2000, the proportion of manufacturing workers had dropped to 15 percent (and many of these workers were not production employees but designers, engineers, marketing executives, and accountants working for manufacturing companies).

Trends in manufacturing jobs (Table 2.16) reveal that deindustrialization hit inelastic areas hard. Though manufacturing's share of employment dropped steadily since 1950, the number of industrial jobs grew in almost all metro areas until the early 1970s. Between 1969 and 1999 the zero-elasticity group lost 2.4 million manufacturing jobs (a devastating −40 percent drop). The low-elasticity group also dropped significantly (−23 percent), but manufacturing jobs increased in medium-, high-, and hyper-elasticity metro areas. For all 119 metro areas, manufacturing employment slid downward from 13.2 million to 11.2 million jobs (a loss of about −15 percent).

Clearly, there is a regional pattern here. Is the deindustrialization of one part of the country and the modest industrialization of another part a simple Frost Belt-Sun Belt phenomenon? In part, yes. Most of the old, smokestack industries that were driven out of business by international competition were located

Box 2.4 Housing Policy *Is* School Policy

In 1966, sociologist James Coleman released his path-breaking study, *Equality of Educational Opportunity.* Sponsored by the then-U.S. Office of Education, the Coleman Report concluded that the socioeconomic characteristics of a child and of the child's classmates (measured principally by family income and parental education) were the overwhelming factors that accounted for academic success. Nothing else—expenditures per pupil, pupil-teacher ratios, teacher experience, instructional materials, age of school buildings, etc.—came close.

"The educational resources provided by a child's fellow students," Coleman summarized, "are more important for his achievement than are the resources provided by the school board." So important are fellow students, the report found, that "the social composition of the student body is more highly related to achievement, independent of the student's own social background, than is any school factor."[1]

In the four decades since, nothing has changed. There has been no more consistent finding of educational researchers—and no research finding more consistently ignored by most politicians and many educators. They will not challenge the underlying racial and class structure of American society.

I have conducted a dozen such studies myself, charting the dominant impact of socioeconomic status on school results. The

TABLE 2.16

INELASTIC REGIONS WERE HARDER HIT BY
DEINDUSTRIALIZATION OF AMERICAN LABOR MARKET

Metro area	Manufacturing jobs as percentage of total jobs 1969	Percentage change in number of manufacturing jobs 1969–1999	Percentage change in number of manufacturing jobs 1989–1999	Manufacturing jobs as percentage of total jobs 1999
Zero Elasticity	24%	–40%	–15%	10%
Low Elasticity	27	–23	–9	13
Medium Elasticity	19	28	6	10
High Elasticity	21	18	1	11
Hyper Elasticity	15	65	6	9

most recent is my study of all elementary schools in Madison-Dane County, Wisconsin. That study finds that

- pupil socioeconomic status accounts for 64 percent to 77 percent of the school-by-school variation in standardized test results and that
- poor children's test results improve dramatically when surrounded by middle-class classmates. Moving a poor child from a neighborhood school where 80 percent of classmates are also poor to a neighborhood school where 80 percent of classmates are middle class would raise the chances of that child's scoring at proficient or advanced levels by 30 to 48 percentage points—an enormous improvement.

In other words, where a child lives largely shapes the child's educational opportunities—not in terms of how much money is being spent per pupil but who the child's classmates are. Housing policy *is* school policy.

1. Quoted in Richard D. Kahlenberg, *All Together Now: Creating Middle-Class Schools through Public School Choice* (Washington, D.C., Brookings Institution Press, 2001), 28. Kahlenberg's thirty-three pages of footnotes to chapters 3 and 4 catalog most major studies on the effects of racial and economic school integration.

in the Northeast or industrial Midwest. Jobs in certain industries (for example, steel and aluminum), once lost, are rarely re-created elsewhere in the country.

In large part, however, the growth in manufacturing in the South and West was not based on export products but on goods that serve primarily growing local markets (for example, bakeries, dairy products, and printing). And even when the number of factory jobs grew, the relative importance of manufacturing in the local economic declined in over 90 percent of metro areas.[6]

Urban areas, however, are not simply passive beneficiaries or victims of economic changes. Local areas can shape their futures. Detroit, for example, may have lost massive numbers of auto industry jobs, but other areas of the country have added automotive jobs (for example, Arlington, Texas, in the Dallas-Ft. Worth

---

Box 2.5 *The Rise of the Creative Class*

"Why cities without gays and rock bands are losing the economic development race." The subtitle of the May 2002 *Washington Monthly* article summarizing Richard Florida's new book, *The Rise of the Creative Class*, is certainly eye catching.[1] And his explanation is thought provoking.

"Talented people seek an environment open to differences," Florida writes. "Many highly creative people, regardless of ethnic background or sexual orientation, grew up feeling like outsiders, different in some way from their classmates. When they are sizing up a new company and community, acceptance of diversity and of gays in particular is a sign that reads 'non-standard people welcome here.'"

And rock bands? "The [creative people] I talked to also desired nightlife with a wide mix of options. The most highly valued options were experiential ones—interesting music venues, neighborhood art galleries, performance spaces, and theaters. A vibrant, varied nightlife was viewed by many as another signal that a city 'gets it,' even by those who infrequently partake in nightlife. More than anything, the creative class craves real experiences in the real world."

"The creative class," Florida argues, "[is] a fast growing, highly educated, and well-paid segment of the workforce on whose efforts corporate profits and economic growth increasingly depend. Members of the creative class do a wide variety of work in a wide variety of industries—from technology to entertainment, journalism to finance, high-end manufacturing to the arts. . . . Places that succeed in attracting creative class people prosper; those that don't fail."

Florida develops a Creativity Index with a mix of four equally weighted factors that ranks all metro areas: creative class share of

---

area; Smyrna, Tennessee, in the Nashville-Murfreesboro area; or Greenville-Spartanburg, South Carolina). An aging plant may be closed as obsolete, but its home region need not lose its replacement. Moreover, an area can certainly nurture or compete for new businesses, based on new types of products and new types of services, which are the basis of most new export jobs.[7]

Each region has attractions in terms of the lifestyle it can offer. The Sun Belt does not have an inherent advantage over the

the workforce; percentage of high-tech industry; innovation, as measured by patents per capita; and diversity, measured by the Gay Index (see <http://www.creativeclass.org>).

Among giant metro areas (1,000,000 or more residents) the top ranked is (not surprisingly) the San Francisco Bay Area, followed by Austin, San Diego, Boston, and Seattle. The bottom five (of 49) are Louisville, Buffalo, Las Vegas, Norfolk-Virginia Beach-Newport News, and Memphis.

For large metro areas (500,000 to 1,000,000), Albuquerque is top-ranked, while Youngstown-Warren ranks last. Among medium-size metro areas (250,000 to 500,000) Madison is number 1; Shreveport brings up the rear. Santa Fe (with both a vigorous cultural scene and Los Alamos National Laboratory) heads the list of small metro areas (50,000 to 250,000) while Enid, Oklahoma, ranks last in the Creativity Index rankings.

"While it is important to have a solid business climate," Florida counsels, "having an effective people climate is even more essential. By this I mean a general strategy aimed at attracting and retaining people—especially, but not limited to, creative people. This entails remaining open to diversity and actively working to cultivate it, and investing in the lifestyle amenities that people really want and use often [urban parks, bike lanes, performance venues], as opposed to using financial incentives to attract companies, build professional sports stadiums, or develop retail complexes."

1. Richard Florida, *The Rise of the Creative Class and How It's Transforming Work, Leisure, Community, and Everyday Life* (New York: Basic Books, 2002). All quotes are from the *Washington Monthly*.

Frost Belt. Many older cities, for example, have cultural facilities and institutions that are superior to those in newer cities. Climate and geography are matters of taste and adjustment. Inelastic areas are not without intrinsic competitive advantages.

Where many inelastic areas have declined is in the ability to compete. Business seeks out labor markets and economic regions, rarely specific governmental jurisdictions. But economic development is a private-public partnership, and the capabilities of the public partner are vital. Typically, a strong, healthy, elastic central city is a metropolitan area's dominant and most capable public partner. This type of city has broad planning and zoning powers (often with extraterritorial planning jurisdiction) and often directly owns major infrastructure systems (e.g., water supply and sewage treatment). With its broad tax base, an elastic city can finance the public infrastructure needed to support major private investment. And it has the power to make major decisions. As Harvey Gannt, former mayor of hyper-elastic Charlotte, observed, metro areas "with fewer governmental entities have a definite advantage in quicker decision making, building regional consensus, and moving forward on large initiatives."[8]

By contrast, who speaks and acts politically for greater Detroit or greater Cleveland, areas suffering from high political fragmentation, strong racial divisions, sharp income differentials, inter-jurisdictional competition—in short, from the loss of a shared sense of community and common destiny metrowide?

Table 2.17 summarizes the rates of job creation in nonmanufacturing occupations. As with comparing rates of population growth, allowances must be made for the different bases on which growth rates are calculated. Nevertheless, more elastic regions (generally, in the South and West) have outperformed less elastic regions (generally, in the Northeast and Midwest) by substantial margins. Even during the 1990s, with the flowering of the Information Age economy, more elastic areas had double the rates of nonmanufacturing job creation. This raises the old chicken or egg dilemma: which came first—new jobs or new people?

An even more complex picture is presented in Table 2.18, which shows the rate of growth in inflation-adjusted per capita personal income metrowide over a thirty-year period (1969–99). The analyses presented to this point would suggest that growth in real incomes should be least in zero-elasticity areas and scale steadily upward to the highest rates in hyper-elasticity areas. Instead, with 29 percent growth in real per capita personal income, the zero-elasticity group outperformed the low-elasticity group (23 percent) and the medium-elasticity group (26 percent). Zero-elastic regions did lag behind the most elastic metro areas (35 percent for both high- and hyper-elasticity areas).

Closer examination shows that average real income growth for the zero-elasticity group was buoyed by the powerful economic performances of America's flagship, postindustrial regions, in the corridor from Boston to Washington, D.C. Tradi-

TABLE 2.17
ELASTIC AREAS HAD FASTER RATES OF NONFACTORY
JOB CREATION THAN INELASTIC AREAS

	Total nonmanufacturing job growth 1969–1999	Total nonmanufacturing job growth 1989–1999
Zero Elasticity	66%	13%
Low Elasticity	92	17
Medium Elasticity	177	32
High Elasticity	168	34
Hyper Elasticity	191	37

tional downtowns prospered as national and international centers of financial, information, government, and business services. Close-in, historic neighborhoods were revived by thousands of young professionals and empty nesters moving in, seeking the cultural vitality of city life (and no commuting to their high-tech jobs in the city's office towers, universities, and medical complexes). Around the outlying beltways other Information Age businesses blossomed. As metropolitan regions, New York, Boston, and San Francisco and their brethren maintained their national economic leadership.

By the end of the 1990s, metropolitan poverty levels had dropped, reaching historic lows for blacks and Hispanics. The lives of too many poor city residents, however, were still un-

TABLE 2.18
ELASTIC AREAS SHOWED GREATER REAL
INCOME GAINS THAN INELASTIC AREAS

	Percentage growth in real per capita personal income 1969–1999	Percentage growth in real per capita personal income 1989–1999
Zero Elasticity	29%	14%
Low Elasticity	23	15
Medium Elasticity	26	14
High Elasticity	35	16
Hyper Elasticity	35	17

touched by the decade's prosperity. Lacking necessary skills and ready transportation, many residents of inelastic cities did not benefit from downtown office jobs (skill barriers) or beltway-centered, service and retail jobs (transportation barriers). Gaps between income classes tended to grow wider within such regions.

From city hall's perspective, municipal bond ratings remain a key indicator of a city's long-term economic health (Table 2.19). Although zero-elasticity cities are in the wealthiest metro areas (at least, nominally), they have bond ratings that are lower than their municipal counterparts in other categories. In 2000, the average bond rating of zero-elasticity cities (A3) was three steps below the average rating of medium-, high-, and hyper-elasticity cities (Aa3).

The Point of (Almost) No Return

Table 2.20 focuses on twenty-four cities that, by 1990, had passed a point of no return that I had defined in the original edition of *Cities without Suburbs*. All twenty-four cities had experienced major population loss (−20 percent or more), had a disproportionate minority population (typically, three, four, five, or more times the percentage of minorities in the suburbs) and, most important, their residents had average income levels that were less than 70 percent of suburban income levels. I called it a point of no return because, through the 1990 census, despite redevelopment projects, enterprise zones, and neighborhood empowerment programs, *no city past the point of no return had ever closed*

TABLE 2.19
ELASTIC CITIES HAVE BETTER BOND
RATINGS THAN INELASTIC CITIES

Central city	City bond rating score	City bond rating (average)
Zero Elasticity	5.44	A3
Low Elasticity	6.61	A1
Medium Elasticity	7.32	Aa3
High Elasticity	7.67	Aa3
Hyper Elasticity	7.63	Aa3

Scale: Aaa = 10.0; Aa1 = 8.5; Aa2 = 8.0; Aa3 = 7.5; A1 = 6.5; A2 = 6.0; A3 = 5.5; Baa1 = 4.5; Baa2 = 4.0; Baa3 = 3.5; Ba1 = 2.5; Ba2 = 2.0; Ba3 = 1.5
Source: Moody's Investor Services

the economic gap with its suburbs by as much as a single percentage point! During the 1980s, all twenty-four cities lost economic ground to their suburbs. In twelve of the twenty-four—Holyoke, Flint, Birmingham, Saginaw, Youngstown, Atlantic City, East Chicago, Gary, Detroit, Trenton, Benton Harbor, and North Chicago—the income gap expanded at disastrous, double-digit rates. Overall, the income levels of the twenty-four cities dropped from 68 percent to 58 percent of suburban levels during the 1980s.

However, as a result of the past decade's economic boom, perhaps the list should be renamed "Cities Past the Point of (*almost*) No Return." During the 1990s, eleven of twenty-four cities did close the income gap with their suburbs (Table 2.20). Chicago (decisively) and Holyoke (just barely) actually escaped the list.

Chicago can justly lay claim to being a comeback city. After four decades of losing population, through large Hispanic immigration Chicago regained over 100,000 residents. More notable was Chicago's resurging average income that rose from 66.2 percent of suburban levels in 1989 to 71.5 percent in 1999. Closing the income gap was due to construction of thousands of new, middle-class townhouses around the Loop, conversion of several massive public housing projects into mixed-income communities, effective work by neighborhood revitalization groups, and, most importantly, an economic boom that, toward the late 1990s, finally cut unemployment and raised incomes in many inner-city neighborhoods.

Collecting income data for 1999, Census 2000 caught the 1990s economic boom at its very peak, the best possible moment for most cities. Few troubled cities saw their relative incomes plummet as occurred in the 1970s and 1980s. Most cities, such as Philadelphia, Detroit, Baltimore, Cleveland, St. Louis, and Buffalo, saw the income gap with their suburbs move up or down by only two or three percentage points.

However, despite some sub-urbanization of middle-class minorities, the concentration of blacks and Hispanics increased substantially in all cities. Overall, blacks and Hispanics constituted 69 percent of the population of the twenty-four cities—over six times their suburban levels. And twenty-one of twenty-four cities continued to lose overall population.

In addition, another twelve central cities passed all three milestones during the 1990s and joined the Cities Past the Point of (almost) No Return list (Table 2.21).[9] And, by 2000, eighteen

TABLE 2.20
WHAT HAPPENED TO 24 CITIES PAST POINT OF (ALMOST) NO RETURN IN 1990s?

City	Population loss since population peak by 1990	Population loss since population peak by 2000	Black and Hispanic percentage of population in 1990	Black and Hispanic percentage of population in 2000	City-suburb ratio of black and Hispanic population in 2000 (3 to 1, etc)	City income as percentage of suburban income in 1989	City income as percentage of suburban income in 1999
			Escaped Point of (Almost) No Return				
CHICAGO, IL	–23%	–20%	60%	63%	3	66.2%	71.5%
Holyoke, MA	–26	–34	35	46	8	69.3	71.4
			Closed Economic Gap with Suburbs				
ATLANTIC CITY, NJ	–43	–39	69	71	3.8	61.0	67.6
DAYTON, OH	–31	–37	36	46	5.2	64.1	66.3
YOUNGSTOWN, OH	–44	–51	35	50	10.8	63.9	64.5
GARY, IN	–25	–42	85	90	8.9	59.1	60.8
CLEVELAND, OH	–45	–48	50	59	4.8	53.5	55.5
DETROIT, MI	–44	–49	77	88	10.4	52.8	53.5
East St Louis, IL	–50	–62	98	99	6.9	39.8	46.0

City							
BENTON HARBOR, MI	-33	-42	93	94	6.7	42.5	43.2
North Chicago, IL	-26	-24	47	56	4.6	37.7	40.7
City-Suburb Economic Gap Still Widening							
FLINT, MI	-29	-37	52	58	6	68.9	68.6
BIRMINGHAM, AL	-22	-29	64	76	5.6	69.2	67.7
ST LOUIS, MO	-54	-59	50	54	3.8	66.9	66.0
BUFFALO, NY	-43	-50	37	46	12	68.9	65.9
SAGINAW, MI	-29	-37	50	57	6.5	65.9	64.5
BALTIMORE, MD	-23	-31	60	67	3.9	64.3	63.0
PHILADELPHIA, PA	-23	-27	45	53	3.4	64.2	60.0
East Chicago, IN	-41	-44	81	88	8.7	59.7	57.2
NEW HAVEN, CT	-21	-25	47	61	6.3	62.3	51.0
HARTFORD, CT	-21	-31	66	81	7.9	53.1	46.3
TRENTON, NJ	-31	-33	59	75	4.7	50.3	45.4
NEWARK, NJ	-38	-38	82	84	3.1	41.7	40.1
Camden, NJ	-30	-36	86	94	6	38.6	36.0
Means for 24 cities	-33	-39	61	69	6.3	57.7	57.2

Notes: A city in uppercase letters is considered to be the primary or historic central city for that metro area. A city in lowercase letters is considered to be a secondary city. All metro areas are defined as they were for the 1990 census. Only Chicago, North Chicago, and Atlantic City gained population (entirely from Hispanic immigration). Proportion of blacks and Hispanics increased from 1 to 15 percentage points in all 24 cities.

TABLE 2.21
12 New Cities Passed Point of (Almost) No Return by 2000

City	Population loss since peak population by 1990	Population loss since peak population by 2000	Black and Hispanic percentage of population in 1990	Black and Hispanic percentage of population in 2000	City-suburb ratio of black and Hispanic population in 2000	City income as percentage of suburban income in 1989	City income as percentage of suburban income in 1999
CANTON, OH	-28%	-31%	19%	24%	8.6	71.1%	69.9%
SYRACUSE, NY	-26	-33	23	33	11.2	76.9	69.8
ELMIRA, NY	-32	-38	14	18	5.2	70.4	69.7
Fall River, MA	-23	-24	3	7	2.7	78.4	69.7
HARRISBURG, PA	-42	-45	57	69	11.5	72.4	69.2
AKRON, OH	-23	-25	25	31	8.9	76.1	68.9
NEW BEDFORD, MA	-18	-23	10	17	7.1	78.1	67.4
ROCHESTER, NY	-30	-34	39	53	9.0	71.1	66.4
PROVIDENCE, RI	-37	-32	28	47	8.6	75.1	66.1
YORK, PA	-30	-32	28	45	16.9	71.4	61.1
Pontiac, MI	-17	-22	50	63	7.4	55.1	57.6
READING, PA	-29	-26	27	51	14.2	70.4	55.7
Means for 12 cities	-28	-30	27	38	9.3	72.2	66.0

Notes: A city in uppercase letters is considered to be the primary or historic central city for that metro area. A city in lowercase letters is considered to be a secondary city. All metro areas are defined as they were for 1990 census. Of 12 cities, only Providence and Reading gained population—increases entirely because of 18–20 percentage point growth of minority population (primarily from Hispanic immigration). Proportion of blacks and Hispanics increased from 4–24 percentage points in all 12 cities.

other central cities had average incomes that had dropped below 70 percent of suburban levels and disproportionate concentrations of minority residents; however, they had not yet lost at least 20 percent of their population. They should be considered on a watch list for Census 2010.[10]

In less flush economic times the continued division of urban America by race and class will throw a dark shadow over the futures of many of these cities.

Cities without Suburbs

The cities in Tables 2.20 and 2.21 are doing very poorly even though many are located in some of the country's nominally wealthiest areas. This section examines the other extreme—cities that are doing well even though they are located in more modest-income metro areas. These are all cities that dominate their areas. They are, in effect, cities without suburbs (Table 2.22).

I have applied two standards to identify a city without suburbs. First, the city must house 50 percent or more of the metro population. On this basis, for example, prominent cities like San Diego, Charlotte, and Houston miss the cut. Second, the average per capita income of city residents must be 90 percent or more of the average per capita income of suburban residents. Below this standard steady suburbanization of the middle class is typically occurring. Lincoln, San Antonio, and Jacksonville, for example, represent more than two-thirds of their metro populations; however, average incomes within the three cities are below 90 percent of suburban levels.

By 2000, only twelve cities still met my cities-without-suburbs criteria (Table 2.22). Three were consolidated governments: Anchorage, Alaska; Lexington-Fayette, Kentucky; and Columbus-Muskogee, Georgia. The others maintained their dominance of the local area through aggressive annexation policies.

Twenty-four other cities almost met the criteria. Eleven had been on the list of cities without suburbs a decade ago, but had not kept pace with suburbanization. One third, however, still had average city incomes above suburban levels. San Antonio, Huntsville, San Diego, Fort Wayne, and, most spectacularly, Lafayette, Louisiana (with a 33 percentage point increase), actually gained ground economically on their suburbs.

TABLE 2.22
TWELVE CITIES WITHOUT SUBURBS

	Percentage of metro residents living in city, 2000	City percentage of suburban per capita income, 1999	Cost-of-living adjusted per capita income of city residents, 1999	Change in adjusted per capita personal income of metro residents, 1969–1999	Residential segregation index for blacks in 2000	Moody's bond rating in 2000
12 Cities without Suburbs						
Anchorage (city and borough), Alaska	100%	100%	$51,816	4%	36	Aa3
Corpus Christi, Tex.	73	116	$45,002	22	44	A3
Colorado Springs, Colo.	70	108	$53,069	39	41	Aa3
Columbus-Muskogee, Ga.	68	99	$50,298	25	58	Aa3
Wichita, Kans.	63	99	$50,441	22	54	Aa2
Albuquerque, N. Mex.	63	112	$45,788	42	32	Aa3
Montgomery, Ala.	61	107	$45,604	43	56	Aa3
Omaha, Nebr.	54	93	$53,760	36	65	Aaa
Lexington-Fayette, Ky.	54	122	$54,892	41	48	Aa2
Tallahassee, Fla.	53	90	$45,939	64	46	A1
Austin, Tex.	53	97	$53,688	70	52	Aa2
Shreveport, La.	51	102	$40,151	31	57	A1
Cities without Suburbs - means	**64**	**104**	**$49,204**	**37**	**49**	**Aa3**
24 Almost-Cities without Suburbs						
Lincoln, Nebr.	90	88	$52,716	27	37	Aa1

San Antonio, Tex.	72	83	$45,402	35	50	Aa2
Jacksonville-Duval, Fla.	67	83	$49,556	38	54	Aa2
Reno, Nev.	53	86	$44,389	25	34	A1
Madison, Wisc.	49	89	$53,813	24	46	Aaa
Indianapolis-Marion, Ind.	49	89	$51,359	30	71	Aaa
Tulsa, Okla.	49	115	$47,920	27	59	Aa2
Houston, Tex.	47	86	$42,797	43	67	Aa3
Oklahoma City, Okla.	47	97	$46,184	15	54	Aa2
Fresno, Calif.	46	96	$33,967	–0	54	A2
Huntsville, Ala.	46	118	$54,930	33	56	Aa2
Columbus, Ohio	46	81	$47,581	33	63	Aaa
Nashville-Davidson, Tenn.	44	93	$51,340	52	57	Aa2
San Diego, Calif.	43	105	$41,780	19	54	Aa1
Modesto, Calif.	42	109	$41,718	2	35	A1
Augusta-Richmond, Ga.	42	84	$41,191	30	45	A2
Fort Wayne, Ind.	41	83	$49,170	23	71	Aa2
Phoenix, Ariz.	41	85	$45,482	28	44	Aa1
Rockford, Ill.	40	90	$46,017	12	63	A1
Fayetteville, N. Car.	40	118	$41,025	38	33	Aa3
Baton Rouge, La.	38	97	$39,005	34	67	A1
Bakersfield, Calif.	37	121	$44,315	–8	52	Aa3
Charlotte, N. Car.	36	122	$56,782	51	55	Aaa
Lafayette, La.	29	149	$48,675	61	51	A2
Almost-Cities without Suburbs - means	**47**	**99**	**$46,546**	**28**	**53**	**Aa2**
83 other major metro areas - means	**28**	**81**	**$38,182**	**29**	**62**	**A1**

Finally, the performance of the remaining eighty-three central cities is summarized on Table 2.22 as well.

None of the cities without suburbs or any of their near-cousins is paradise. None is exempt from the social problems of modern-day America. To the eyes of some residents of the nation's more glamorous and cosmopolitan centers, most of these thirty-six may appear to be modest communities that, in Winston Churchill's words, "have much to be modest about." And yet, both as cities and as whole metro areas they are doing pretty well. With the exception of Anchorage and San Diego, all have average or below average costs of living. This means that their residents' nominal incomes (as reported by the census) stretch farther than higher incomes reported in high-cost regions, such as the Boston-to-Washington corridor or Northern and Southern California.

These two groups dominated their metropolitan areas in 2000, contained 64 percent and 47 percent, respectively, of their regional populations; the other eighty-three central cities contained only 28 percent. Residents of cities without suburbs might be expected to be better off than residents of less elastic cities that are a smaller share of their regions' populations and where many of the wealthy have fled to their suburbs. In 1999, the residents of cities without suburbs had incomes four percent above suburban levels; the residents of almost-cities without suburbs were at parity, while in the other eighty-three cities' average incomes were 19 percent below that of their suburbs.

Adjusted for differences in cost of living, real median family income translated into $49,204 for residents of cities without suburbs, $46,546 for residents of almost-cities without suburbs, and $38,182 for residents of the other eighty-three central cities—a 29 percent higher standard of living for residents of cities without suburbs. The economic strength of these cities was reflected in somewhat better municipal bond ratings (Aa2 and Aa1, respectively); none of the thirty-six cities had less than an A1 rating.

Though not shown in Table 2.22, the average family of the thirty-six metro areas also had slightly higher real median family incomes ($50,484 and $49,339, respectively) than average families in the other eighty-three areas ($49,156), counting all of the latter group's wealthier, more exclusive suburban enclaves. And over a recent thirty-year period (1969–99), the twelve cities without suburbs regions were widening their advantage with an inflation-adjusted growth rate (37 percent) higher than the real growth rate of the eighty-three areas (29 percent). Without the drag of California's three Central Valley communities, the remaining 21 almost-cities without suburbs recorded a real growth rate of 32 percent.

The key, I believe, is that these thirty-six communities are becoming societies of greater social equity and economic mobility. They have lower levels of racial segregation—segregation indices of 49 and 53 compared with 62—still far, however, from being truly integrated societies. Since these cities have greater unity among their public institutions, their residents have better access to their entire region's resources than do residents of more fragmented regions.

In short, however modest cities without suburbs may appear on the world stage, they are making more of their region's available resources. What would happen if more fragmented regions, particularly their inelastic inner cities, could harness the resources and opportunities of their entire regions? Chapter III discusses some of the possibilities.

Notes

1. As noted in the previous chapter, there were actually 541 designated central cities for Census 2000; 20 cities, however, were either too small for data on municipal area to have been reported in 1950 or did not even exist at all!

2. All but a dozen of these 149 smaller metro areas are free-standing areas, not outlying regions of larger metropolitan areas, like Racine, Wisconsin (part of the greater Milwaukee area), and Vineland-Millville-Bridgeton, New Jersey (part of the greater Philadelphia area). Except for many metro areas located in Florida, Texas, and California, these smaller metro areas are relatively slow-growing urban nodes, small manufacturing communities, or commercial centers for agricultural and natural resource regions. In 1950 only 9 out of the 149 areas (Amarillo and Waco, Texas; Asheville, North Carolina; Cedar Rapids, Iowa; Decatur and Springfield, Illinois; Pueblo, Colorado; St. Joseph, Missouri; and Topeka, Kansas) were considered important enough by the Census Bureau to rank as Metropolitan Areas. Most of the 9 have quietly—and perhaps not unhappily—watched the world pass them by.

3. Of course, "White-only metro areas" are not discrimination-free communities. Interestingly, however, none of these central cities has developed a significant income gap with its suburbs in either elastic or inelastic metro areas. In "White America" regions in New England, New York, and Pennsylvania, 16 inelastic cities lost –15 percent of their population while their regions were growing modestly (18 percent). Elsewhere in white America, through annexation, more elastic cities expanded vigorously in area (202 percent) and moderately in population (91 percent) while their regions' populations were growing slightly

faster (102 percent). However, city-to-suburb income percentages ranged from a low of only 83 percent in Johnstown, Pennsylvania, to a high of 123 percent in Boise City, Idaho. The very absence of city-suburb income gaps and the paucity of little boxes suburbs suggest the role that racial issues play as drivers of urban growth patterns and city-suburb disparities in more racially and ethnically diverse metro areas.

4. In the first edition of *Cities without Suburbs* I gave equal weight to initial density and boundary expansion. Through further statistical analysis I found that assigning three times greater importance to boundary expansion better fit a central city's capture/contribute percentage. The effect is to emphasize the importance of annexation and city/county consolidation in a city's relative elasticity ranking.

5. Of 331 metro areas, the only ones to lose population over the fifty years were Jersey City and St. Joseph, Missouri (which both dropped −6 percent), and five coal mining regions: Charleston, West Virginia (−3 percent); Altoona (−7 percent), Scranton-Wilkes Barre (−13 percent), and Johnstown (−20 percent), Pennsylvania; and Wheeling, West Virginia-Ohio (−22 percent).

6. Of 119 metro areas, from 1969 to 1999, the relative share of manufacturing jobs increased only in Austin (8 percent to 10 percent), Colorado Springs (5 percent to 9 percent), Huntsville (12 percent to 16 percent), Lafayette, Louisiana (6 percent to 7 percent), Reno (5 percent to 6 percent), Tucson (6 percent to 8 percent), and Santa Rosa (11 percent to 12 percent) and Vallejo-Fairfield (7 percent to 9 percent), two outliers of the San Francisco Bay Area.

7. At the cost of tremendous subsidies, the city of Detroit did succeed in getting two new assembly plants for 6,000 workers. The Detroit region's true competitive advantage has become its role as a global center of automotive design and engineering.

8. Harvey B. Gannt, "A Tale of Two Cities: Charlotte's Regional Approach Means Fast Decisions, Fast Results, " in "Turning Point," a special section of the *Boston Globe*, October 30, 1994, p. 28.

9. Five more cities—Bessemer, Alabama; Hammond, Indiana; Chicago Heights, Illinois; and McKeesport and Norristown, Pennsylvania—would have also joined the list, but they lost their designation by the federal government as central cities—a more telling measure of their decline than my statistics.

10. Cities on the watch list are Milwaukee; Savannah; Kansas City, Kansas; Lorain, Ohio; Woonsocket, Rhode Island; Petersburg; Bridgeport and Waterbury, Connecticut; Allentown, Lancaster, and Lebanon, Pennsylvania; and Brockton, Fitchburg, Lawrence, Lowell, Lynn, and Springfield, Massachusetts; Alliance, Ohio; New Britain, Connecticut. Elizabeth, Paterson, and Perth Amboy, New Jersey, would be on the watch list but have also been de-designated as central cities.

Chapter III

Strategies for Stretching Cities

Reversing the fragmentation of urban areas is an essential step in ending severe racial and economic segregation. The "city" must be redefined to reunify city and suburb.

Optimally, such reunification is achieved through formally organizing a metropolitan or quasi-metropolitan government (a Big Box). This can be accomplished through formal city-county consolidation, which is, in effect, a type of superannexation by the central city. Steady annexation by the central city can serve much the same goal.

Where city-county consolidation cannot be achieved (which will be in most regions) or annexation is either impossible or becoming more difficult, three key policies must be implemented so that the many "little boxes" will act as a "Big Box." Such functional policies may be termed "elasticity mimics."[1]

Three Essential Regional Policies

City and suburb would be reunified if a metro government adopts (or multiple local governments are required to adopt) three policies:

- Implement regional inclusionary zoning and other mixed-income housing strategies for integrating low-income households into middle-class communities in order to diminish racial and economic segregation and eliminate concentrated poverty;
- implement regional land use and transportation planning and growth management strategies in order to control suburban sprawl and reverse urban disinvestment; and

- implement regional tax-base sharing in order to reduce fiscal imbalances that result from uneven growth and socioeconomic imbalances.

Tax-base sharing alone would be inadequate; no feasible amount of money can salvage isolated inner cities and declining inner suburbs. Unfettered urban sprawl promotes economic segregation and constantly threatens inelastic cities and older suburbs with slow abandonment. Fair share housing programs are slow to take hold and are most effective within a vigorously expanding housing market. All three strategies are inseparable and indispensable parts of a successful approach.

DIMINISH RACIAL AND ECONOMIC SEGREGATION

"Public policy dictates where development occurs," states the National Association of Home Builders (surely no champions of governmental regulation). Through planning and zoning powers, local governments shape what gets built where for whose benefit, affecting, in particular, the local housing market. A broad-based, Big Box government is not generally as afflicted with the Not-in-My-Backyard syndrome as is a narrow-based, little boxes government. A Big Box can carry out inclusionary zoning policies that require private, for-profit homebuilders to create mixed-income rather than economically segregated housing developments (Box 3.1). Also, within its wide jurisdiction, a Big Box can scatter public housing projects and implement rent subsidy programs across many neighborhoods.

That a Big Box would pursue automatically such policies is hardly guaranteed. Nevertheless, it can and does happen. In a highly fragmented metro area, however, the many little boxes will not adopt such politically controversial policies without being compelled to do so by state legislatures or state courts (Box 3.2).

CONTROL SUBURBAN SPRAWL

Suburban sprawl does not just happen as the natural outcome of some unfettered, free market forces. Sprawl is the result of an interlocking complex of federal, state, and local policies that set the framework for private investment. Most state legislatures have delegated broad planning and zoning powers to local governments to regulate land development. If it has the political will, a Big Box can promote more compact development, preserve farmland and natural areas, and encourage reinvestment in older residential and commercial areas (Box 3.3). Within a little boxes region, it is virtually useless (and even perilous) for one little box to undertake such policies by itself. Once again, getting all neighboring little boxes to act as one invariably requires state mandates or very powerful state incentives.

REDUCE FISCAL IMBALANCE

By taxing a larger share of a region's wealth, a Big Box matches resources to problems. A Big Box is implicitly a tax-base sharing mechanism; it taxes richer neighborhoods in order to maintain adequate services in poorer neighborhoods that they could not afford by themselves. In little boxes regions, however, richer and poorer neighborhoods are separate governments unto themselves. Poorer communities have no way of tapping the wealth of richer communities without the intervention of a higher level of government (Box 3.4).

Metro Government: A Definition

Before examining the feasibility of creating metro governments, I need to offer a working definition of what a metro government is. The country abounds with over 34,000 special purpose units of local government (transit authorities, water and sewer agencies, and community college districts, for example). Often they are metrowide. Although creating special purpose governments may be seen as a step toward ultimately achieving metropolitan unification, a true metro government must be a general-purpose local government. It must have all of the powers of a municipality under applicable state law. Moreover, it must exercise exclusive powers over its responsibilities within its jurisdiction. In other words, it must not be a general government that fills in the interstices between a myriad of major municipal enclaves. Such is the situation of many county governments regarding unincorporated land in highly urbanized areas.

A metro government need not be responsible for all local public functions. Special purpose and other local general govern-

---

Box 3.1 Montgomery County: Mixing Up the Neighborhood

Montgomery County, Maryland, has long been renowned as having the nation's most progressive, mixed-income housing policies. The Housing Opportunities Commission (the county's public housing authority and housing finance agency) owns, rents, or administers an inventory of more than 40,000 housing units (most in mixed-income neighborhoods), or about 12 percent of the total housing supply.

One of Montgomery County's key tools is its Moderately Priced Dwelling Unit ordinance. Enacted in 1973, the MPDU law requires private developers to build mixed income housing everywhere. The law covers any new subdivision, townhouse complex, or apartment development with at least 35 housing units.

Under the county law, most of the new housing can be market rate (at whatever income level the builder targets), but at least 12.5 to 15 percent must be affordable housing, or MPDUs. To qualify for an MPDU, a family's income cannot exceed 65 percent of the county's average household income, which was $71,551 in 1999.

To help integrate the poorest households into middle-class society, the county law further specifies that one-third of the MPDUs, or 5 percent of the units built, must be available for rent or purchase by the Housing Opportunities Commission.

Montgomery County never builds public housing projects. It simply buys standard housing scattered all over the county as rental housing for its poorest families.

Complying with the county's ground rules, private home-builders and apartment developers have produced more than 11,000 MPDUs—two-thirds for sale, one-third for rent. Many buyers are local school teachers, county police officers, office workers, supermarket clerks, fast food cooks—in short, the very civil ser-

---

ments can still exist. A metro government, however, must control key planning and zoning powers and housing policy.

Though preferable, a metro government need not cover the entire metro area; it should contain at least 50 percent of the area's population and have within its jurisdiction a substantial amount of undeveloped land. Thus, it can either control much new peripheral development or pursue land conservation policies, promoting more compact development. A metro government must include the region's central city.

vants, retail trade, and service industry workers who serve local communities.

To house welfare recipients and other poor residents, the Housing Opportunities Commission has purchased more than 1,700 of the new MPDUs and rents 1,500 more. (Church groups and private, nonprofits have bought others.) The county-owned units are so scattered that HOC pays annual membership assessments to over 220 private homeowners associations.

The 85-10-5 income mix produces no social problems, according to HOC officials, police, and social agencies, and resale prices of market-rate homes are unaffected by being within mixed income housing developments.

With 873,000 residents in 2000, Montgomery County, Maryland, is a governmental Big Box. In 1927 the Maryland General Assembly gave county government exclusive planning and zoning control throughout most of the county.[1]

Its progressive policies have produced a remarkable social and economic transformation. In 1970 Montgomery County had the look of a classic suburb—wealthy and white (92 percent). By 2000, Montgomery County had a rainbow look—16 percent black, 12 percent Hispanic, 12 percent Asian—and was still the thirteenth wealthiest county in America while becoming one of the nation's more racially and economically integrated communities.

By providing housing for all occupational levels, the county helped promote a diversified local economy centered on its I-270 Technology Corridor. In a generation the Montgomery County has become the global center of biomedical and genetic research.

1. The legislature "grandfathered" existing zoning powers for the cities of Rockville and Gaithersburg and five small villages (about 12 percent of the county's population).

State Government's Crucial Role

Although this book is written from Washington, D.C., it is based on my experiences as a mayor and state legislator. Restructuring local governance is not a national government task. It is primarily the responsibility of citizens and political leaders at local and state levels. State government sets the rules of the game.

America is a federal system. Within the bounds of our national constitution, states have certain sovereign powers. Our

---

Box 3.2 States Push Fair Share Suburban Housing

Although none is as effective as Montgomery County, Maryland's mandatory inclusionary zoning law (Box 3.1), at least three states—Massachusetts, Connecticut, and New Jersey—have enacted state laws making clear that little boxes suburbs cannot exclude affordable housing from their communities.

Massachusetts's antisnob zoning law is the earliest (1969), giving a state adjudicatory commission the power to override local objections to affordable housing proposals. As of 2001, 119 Massachusetts cities and towns had enacted some form of local ordinances either mandating (for example, Cambridge) or providing incentives for building affordable housing.

In 1989, the Connecticut General Assembly passed the Affordable Housing Land-Use Appeals Procedure. If a town rejects a developer's affordable housing proposal, the developer can challenge the local ruling in a special state court. The burden of proof is on the town to prove that its reasons for rejecting the project "clearly outweigh the need for affordable housing."

Production of affordable housing under both Massachusetts and Connecticut's laws rely on builder initiative; only several hundred units are produced a year. However, between 1983 and 2002 almost 29,000 new affordable housing units were built, and more than 11,000 affordable units were rehabilitated in several hundred New Jersey municipalities. Such a level of affordable housing production is mandated by the New Jersey Supreme Court's pathbreaking *Mt. Laurel I* (1977) and *Mt. Laurel II* (1983) decisions and the legislature's subsequent Fair Housing Act of 1985.

On the one hand, that is an impressive achievement. On the other hand, it is less than 5 percent of all new housing units built since 1983 (an estimated 625,000 units). Had Montgomery County's inclusionary zoning formula been in effect in New Jersey, it would have yielded more than 46,000 newly constructed affordable units, or about 60 percent more than the *Mt. Laurel*-Fair Housing Act compliance has produced.

And—a crucial step—were Montgomery County's practice of having its public housing authority acquire one-third of the MP-

---

national constitution is silent on the topic of local government. Under the Tenth Amendment, authority over local government is implicitly reserved to state governments. Local governments (including local school districts) are legally creatures of state

DUs also adopted, thousands of very low-income families would have been integrated into new, overwhelmingly middle-class neighborhoods. Instead, with the exception of older city housing rehabilitated under Regional Contribution Agreements, New Jersey's policies rarely aid desperately needy families. Regional Contribution Agreements allow wealthy suburbs to sell back up to half of their fair share allocation to poor cities. By 2002, almost 8,000 RCA-financed units had been created (primarily through rehabilitation) in high-poverty cities.

RCA proponents argue that suburban fair share targets are higher than they would otherwise be because the cities' needs are factored into the regional formula, that the cities are voluntarily receiving back a portion of their own needs financed by suburban money (about $20,000 a unit), and that, by 2002, RCAs had provided an infusion of over $150 million of outside investment into city housing markets (which undoubtedly leveraged many tens of millions of dollars more).

That is undoubtedly true. However, as of 2000, fifty-seven sending townships averaged almost three times the average income level of the receiving cities and boroughs. The percentage of poor children in the wealthy, sending suburban school districts averaged just 6 percent; the percentage of poor children in the poverty-impacted, receiving city school districts exceeded 71 percent. Whatever else they may have achieved, rather than opening up mainstream opportunities, the RCAs literally cemented 15,000 to 20,000 poor children into poverty-impacted neighborhoods and schools where they were doomed to fail in overwhelming numbers!

In fact, in 2000 New Jersey ranked as having the fifth most segregated elementary schools for blacks (and getting worse), fifth for Hispanics (and getting slightly less bad), and first for segregation of low-income pupils (and getting slightly worse).

New Jersey's fair share policies create affordable shelter mostly for existing suburban residents. They have not advanced the cause of racial and economic justice for inner-city residents.

government. State legislatures frame the standards and procedures by which new municipalities are created. Typically, state governments can do more than merely set the ground rules for local action. State legislatures can also create new local govern-

Box 3.3 Metro Builds Great Wall of Portland

With its urban growth boundary, the Portland region has the USA's most effective—and unique—integrated system of transportation and land use planning.

Its effectiveness is based on the state of Oregon's Land Use Act of 1973 that required Oregon's 36 county governments to adopt sprawl-limiting, comprehensive land use plans that comply with 14 state goals. The county plans incorporate urban growth boundaries for Oregon's 242 municipalities that clearly divide urban from rural land.

Its uniqueness rests in the fact that, for the complex, highly urbanized Portland region, Portland Metro, the country's only directly elected regional government, is the regional planning agency. Until 2003, Metro was governed by an elected chief executive and seven-member council elected directly from the seven districts into which the region is divided. (None can be elected officials of other governments.)[1]

Metro is not an all-purpose government. It does not replace the three county and twenty-four municipal governments within its region. Metro is a special purpose government, established by the Oregon legislature and the region's voters explicitly to be the regional planning agency.

Periodically, Metro has been assigned responsibility for certain regional services, such as the Oregon Zoo, the Oregon Convention Center, the regional parks system, and a regional solid waste disposal and recycling system. These are major functions in terms of Metro's current $303 million budget and 732 employees in fiscal year 2003. However, they are minor functions compared with Metro's planning powers to shape the region's future.

Adopted in 1979, the regional urban growth boundary (UGB) originally contained 342 square miles. Metro expanded the UGB by six square miles in 1998. The UGB draws a clear line between

a) land preserved exclusively for farming, forestry, and wilderness and recreation areas (no urbanization is allowed), and
b) land that would be urbanized. Inside the UGB, sufficient land must be provided for twenty years of anticipated residential, commercial, and industrial growth.

In 2000, over 1.3 million people (more than 95 percent of the population of the three-county region, lived within the 348 square mile UGB. The remaining population lived in smaller towns and rural areas in the remaining 2,662 square miles outside the UGB.

One measure of the UGB's effectiveness is its success in protecting farmland. During the 1990s, for example, the region's population grew 17.6 percent, but only 0.1 percent of its farmland was urbanized. Planning ahead, Metro expects that a 50 percent increase in population by 2040 will only require urbanization of about 2,500 acres of current farmland.

Another measure of the UGB's effectiveness is the region's balanced economic and social health. By preventing new development from occurring outward, the UGB focuses much private investment inward into the central city and older suburbs. The Portland region is one of the USA's most ethnically and economically integrated societies. The city of Portland is a growing, Aaa-credit rated central city. And none of Portland's twenty-three suburban municipalities is fiscally or socially distressed.

Winston Churchill once said: "We first shape our buildings. Then our buildings shape us."

For thirty years Oregonians have been shaping their building—the Oregon Land Use Act, state oversight agencies, and Portland Metro. A dozen times since 1978, voters of the region have gone to the polls to elect the Metro Council and Executive Officer. Land use and transportation planning controversies are always the election issues.

Beyond the governmental institutions, Oregon has developed a powerful citizens lobby, 1,000 Friends of Oregon, that serves as a watchdog over the entire process. 1,000 Friends of Oregon has defended good planning principles and citizens' rights to be involved many times in planning decisions.

That intensely democratic process has, in turn, reshaped the builders. There is broader and more knowledgeable citizen involvement in land use planning issues in Oregon (particularly, within Portland Metro communities) than in any other area of the USA.[2]

To the extent that Oregonians are different, their institutions have helped to educate and shape them.

1. After approving a charter change in 2002, regional voters now elect the president of the Metro Council. The Council, in turn, hires a chief administrator.
2. Oregon voters, however, are not immune to conservative-inspired ballot initiatives, such as the so-called property rights amendment adopted in 2000.

ments and merge old ones (including school districts)—often without any constitutional requirement for local voter approval. However, after consolidating over 108,000 local school districts (as of 1942) into less than 16,000 larger, more unified districts (by 1972), legislatures have rarely exercised such powers since.

Governors and state legislators can and do act as metrowide policymakers. There are instances when state governments have mandated areawide local cooperation in a range of functional activities (transportation planning, sewage treatment, air quality control, senior citizens programs) or (much more rarely) regional tax-base sharing or fair share affordable housing programs.

State government also plays an increasingly important role in revenue sharing for local government and, above all, for local school systems. By 2000 state aid had grown to 20 percent of city and county government revenues. By the 1999–00 school year state governments were providing 50 percent of local school districts' budgets. With the purse comes additional power (and responsibility) to provide for the more rational and equitable organization of metro areas.

Statutory authority aside, however, why should governors and state legislators have any greater political opportunity to implement unpopular reforms? Are they not elected by the same voters as local officials?

Governors, of course, have statewide constituencies, and most state legislative districts are not coterminous with local government jurisdictions. Moreover, there is a tendency to view central cities and suburbs as monolithic blocks automatically opposed to each other. (This book is guilty of that perspective.) In reality, there is tremendous variety among central cities (which I have tried to illustrate) and among suburban communities as well.

Suburban diversity is the key to building effective political coalitions in state legislatures. Both inelastic central cities and older, often blue-collar, suburbs are victimized by typical regional growth patterns that focus most high-end residential and commercial development in newer suburbs. Indeed, when inner-city problems begin to grow rapidly in older, blue-collar suburbs, these communities often have fewer resources to combat rising poverty, crime, and other problems than central cities. Central cities and older suburbs are potentially allied by mutual self-interest, and the state legislature is the arena in which bonds can be forged (Box 3.5).

Box 3.4 Twin Cities Region Shares Tax Base

The Mall of America, the USA's biggest, sits in suburban Bloomington, Minnesota. Yet every one of 186 municipalities and over 100 school districts and special authorities in the 7-county Minneapolis-St. Paul region shares in the millions of dollars in tax revenues generated by the giant mall.

Why? The Twin Cities Fiscal Disparities Plan, the nation's largest regional tax-base sharing program.

Enacted in 1971 by the Minnesota legislature, the plan pools 40 percent of the increase in all communities' commercial/industrial property valuation. All cities and townships keep their pre-1971 tax bases plus 60 percent of the annual growth. The pool is then taxed at a uniform rate and redistributed among all local government entities.

The redistribution formula estimates each community's annual population and how its commercial/industrial tax base per capita compares with the regional per capita average. Poorer than average communities receive more back from the fund than they contribute. Richer than average communities contribute more than they receive.

By 2000 the annual Fiscal Disparities fund amounted to $407 million, over 28 percent of all commercial/industrial property taxes collected. Some 137 municipalities were net recipients; 49 were net contributors. The net contributors were primarily wealthy suburbs lying in the Fertile Crescent southwest of the Twin Cities. Giant malls, office towers, and gardenlike industrial parks have sprouted along the interstate highways that border these suburbs or adjacent to the suburban Minneapolis–St. Paul International Airport.

The tax-base sharing program narrows fiscal disparities between rich and poor communities. Without the plan, the tax-base disparity would be 17 to 1. The Fiscal Disparities Plan narrows the gap to 4 to 1 between richest and poorest.

Township States vs. County States

How local governance is organized in different states has a big impact on central city elasticity and on the degree to which city-county consolidation and annexation are feasible strategies. New England, New York, New Jersey, and Pennsylvania are com-

---

Box 3.5 *Metropolitics:* **USA in Red, Orange, and Blue**

"We're spending too much time flirting with Blue Land," the community organizer said in a staff meeting. "We need to do more hard, grassroots organizing in Orange Land to add to our base in Red Land."

Blue Land? Red Land? *Orange* Land? This is not some variation on network television's Election Night coverage. It's a new tool for understanding metropolitan America—multicolored maps.

The maps are the creation of Myron Orfield. Now a full-time champion of regionalism, as a Minnesota legislator Orfield forged the first enduring alliance in America between declining central cities and older, threatened, blue-collar suburbs.

Orfield also pioneered the use of a political tool: maps that, jurisdiction by jurisdiction, trace the decline of central cities (colored red) and many older, inner-ring suburbs (colored orange), and the rise of affluent outer-ring suburbs (colored blue).

He told this story first in *Metropolitics: A Regional Agenda for Community and Stability* (Brookings Institution Press, 1997), largely a case study of the Twin Cities region. Through the work of his Metropolitan Area Research Corporation, Orfield has now mapped dozens of metropolitan regions, spreading his doctrine of metropolitics. His work in the twenty-five largest metropolitan

---

pletely divided into incorporated cities, towns and villages, and townships (Box 3.6). There is no unincorporated land for their cities to annex. Most midwestern states are also totally divided into townships, but a township's legal status varies from state to state. In recent decades, Michigan townships, for example, have wielded strong political power; most have resisted annexation successfully. By contrast, townships in Indiana exist primarily to tax local property owners for indigent relief and play no role in annexation decisions. A band of twenty "township states" (that is, little boxes states) extends north of the Ohio River from Maine to North Dakota.

The rest of the country is made up of "county states" (or Big Box states) where urbanized islands exist as incorporated cities, towns, and villages in the midst of a sea of unincorporated land. For unincorporated areas, county government serves as a kind

areas is summarized in *American Metropolitics: The New Suburban Reality* (Brookings Institution Press, 2002).

A few academicians and journalists had pointed out how urban poverty was spreading from inner city to inner suburbs, but Orfield has developed the most compelling and comprehensive documentation of this trend and has translated it into effective political action.

Metropolitics teaches that making progress on hard, divisive issues such as controlling sprawl, creating mixed-income housing, or tax-base sharing is rarely based on friendly, consensual agreement, but more often on building political coalitions. In highly fragmented, little boxes regions only state legislatures can serve as regional policy bodies, setting new ground rules for how myriad local governments must share common responsibilities for common problems. Those coalitions are most durable when based on each member's political self-interest. The glue that held the Minnesota legislative coalition together was underlying social, economic, and political self-interest.

Orfield's maps graphically portray that underlying self-interest are getting city and suburban politicians to see beyond traditional racial division and past history to a common agenda. The emerging central city-older suburbs alliance is America's best hope for changing the rules of the game.

---

of general-purpose government, although it typically offers a less intensive level of services than would a municipal government. With the exception of Virginia's system of independent cities, municipal annexation does not remove an area from a county's overall jurisdiction so county governments often support municipal annexations.

ENCOURAGE CITY-COUNTY CONSOLIDATION

Typically, movements to create areawide governmental units have focused on consolidating municipal governments with their surrounding county governments. In recent decades the most notable consolidations have merged the central city with single counties. Indianapolis-Marion County, Nashville-Davidson County, and Jacksonville-Duval County are examples (Box 3.7).

Box 3.6 Northern Tier States Fragmented by Townships

There are 16,666 townships recorded in the Census of Governments, covering 20 northern states. In New England, New York, New Jersey, and Pennsylvania, towns and townships originated in colonial times. But why does this system exist in most of the Midwest? Blame it on Thomas Hutchins.

Thomas Hutchins was a British engineer captain in the 60th Royal Regiment stationed at Fort Pitt (Pittsburgh) at the end of the French and Indian War in 1764. Hutchins proposed surveying the vast Ohio Territory that had come to victorious England from defeated France. He would divide the wilderness into townships 6 miles square and further subdivide townships into 160-acre sections. British Army veterans would be allotted sections of western lands as a bonus for their military service.

Nothing came immediately of Hutchins's plan, but Hutchins had the good judgment (or good luck) to stick around and throw in his lot with the rebellious colonists a decade later. At the end of our War for Independence, the Continental Congress (under the Articles of Confederation) adopted Hutchins's plan as the Land Ordinance of 1785 and appointed him first Geographer of the United States to implement it. Congress's motivation was the same as Hutchins's original intent; pay off veterans of the Continental Army with western lands. (The biggest beneficiary was General George Washington, who claimed over 50,000 acres near the future Columbus, Ohio.) As the different territories (Ohio, Indiana, Michigan, etc.) became states, their constitutions converted congressional townships into local units of government.

Whatever townships' value in civilizing the 19th-century frontier, for the 21st century the overall effect is the atomization of local government. With 2,745 local general governments, for example, Minnesota has one government for every 1,800 residents. Illinois, with 102 counties, 1,282 municipalities, and 1,433 townships (not to mention its 997 independent school districts and another 2,995 special districts) is the champion of microgovernment.

The New England town meeting is enshrined in the American myth, and the National Association of Towns and Townships proudly proclaims itself the champion of "hometown government" and "grassroots government." However, township states contain most of the most racially and economically segregated metro areas in the nation, and local communities' ability to compete economically is constantly constrained by the absence of governance structures to pull together regional resources.

Box 3.7 Urban Body Building in Louisville-Jefferson County

In an exercise of what one noted commentator called urban body building, Louisville and Jefferson County consolidated on January 1, 2003. It was the largest city-county consolidation in thirty-three years.

Local voters had twice rejected consolidation, most recently in 1983. What caused the turnaround in public sentiment for the 2000 election?

In a word, probably jealousy.

Forty years ago, when Louisville's population was at its peak (390,639), Louisville competed fiercely with the city of Indianapolis (476,258) that lies some 110 miles north on Interstate 65. Louisville lorded it over Nashville (170,874) and rarely took notice of farther-off Jacksonville (201,810). Lexington (62,810) was simply the small-town home of the University of Kentucky Wildcats, arch-rivals of the hometown Louisville Cardinals.

Forty years later, Indianapolis, Nashville, and Jacksonville had doubled or tripled inelastic Louisville's population. With the National Football League Colts, Titans, and Jaguars, all three cities also literally achieved big-league status while Louisville remained a college town.

Perhaps as galling to Louisville's pride, by 2000, even once-lowly Lexington (260,512) had pushed Louisville (256,321) aside as Kentucky's biggest city.

The key for all four competitors was city-county consolidation: Nashville-Davidson (1963), Jacksonville-Duval (1968), Indianapolis-Marion (1970), and Lexington-Fayette (1973). Absorbing existing suburban population (and plenty of land to grow on), these consolidated entities could instantly market themselves as big cities.

Since the Census Bureau lists consolidated city-counties as municipalities, consolidated Louisville (693,604) jumped from the 67th largest city to the 16th largest. (If the population of Jefferson County's 93 other unmerged municipalities are deducted, the consolidated city of about 531,000 residents ranks 28th.)

The consolidated government is headed by a mayor and 26-member council elected by district. They face many typical urban problems, but an expanded tax base and beefed-up identity are new tools to work with.

1. Alan Ehrenhalt, "Secrets of Urban Bodybuilding," *Governing Magazine* (January 2001).

Each city-county consolidation has been (and must be) cus-
tom-made for its area. The final structure should represent a
compromise, balancing good government idealism, tradition,
and political realities. Traditional functions of county government may be absorbed into the newly unified government
(Nashville-Davidson) or may be continued as independent functions while the new government assumes service-providing
functions for all unincorporated areas (Indianapolis-Marion
County). Bowing to political reality, certain municipal enclaves
may remain in existence (for example, Baldwin and the three
beaches within Jacksonville-Duval County), and rural residents
may have to be assured that consolidation will not mean an au-
tomatic increase in taxes through maintaining a lower service,
lower tax zone (Nashville's General Services District).

Despite such compromises, most city-county consolidations
do initially achieve the key goals of adding more developable
land, population, and tax base to the central city. Absent such
elastic effects, however, consolidation just eliminates one level of
government. That was the result when Kansas City, Kansas, having previously annexed all remaining land within Wyandotte
County, consolidated with what had become a redundant
county government. Similarly, in little boxes New York State,
consolidating Rochester with Monroe County or Buffalo with
Erie County, for instance, would have no city-stretching effects.
None of Rochester's twenty-nine or Buffalo's forty-two neighboring cities and towns would likely consolidate into the new
entity.[2] The two cities would be swapping their elected mayors
and city councils for elected country executives and county legislatures with little or no net increase in resources for the central
cities.

With the continued spread of suburbia and long-distance commuting, the consolidated cities' long-term dilemma is that metro
areas steadily grow beyond their new boundaries. Indianapolis-
Marion County, Nashville-Davidson County, and Jacksonville-
Duval County were all highly successful consolidations of the
1960s. Today Indianapolis-Marion County's population is only
49 percent of its ten-county metro area; Nashville-Davidson, 44
percent of its six-county area; and Jacksonville-Duval County, 67
percent of its four-county area. To maintain city-county consolidation's benefits, these multicounty regions must adopt strong,
antisprawl growth management policies.

POTENTIAL IMPACT OF CITY-COUNTY CONSOLIDATION

City-county consolidations have been relatively rare—only twenty-five since World War II. In fact, only fourteen states have specific statutes authorizing city-county consolidation and setting forth the procedures for its achievement (Table 3.1). Of the fourteen states, six are in the West, five in the South, three in the Midwest, and none in the Northeast, where counties often hardly exist as meaningful governmental units. Eleven of the fourteen states require various forms of local referendums. (The exceptions are California, Utah, and Virginia.)

The absence of authorizing legislation, however, does not preclude most legislatures from implementing specific city-county consolidations as legislative acts. Such, indeed, was the path followed successfully in consolidating Indianapolis-Marion County as well as, a century ago, in creating New York City (Box 1.2).

Table 3.2 projects what might be the hypothetical impact of city-county consolidation. It divides the country into four groups. In group 0, city-county consolidations are impossible or, rather, highly unlikely to occur (at least, within my lifetime or,

TABLE 3.1
STATE LAWS REGARDING CITY-COUNTY CONSOLIDATION

	Number of states				Total
State law	South [16]	West [13]	Midwest [12]	Northeast [9]	USA [50]
Consolidation of cities and counties is authorized	5	6	3	0	14
Referendum and majority approval of each city affected is required	1	3	2	0	6
Referendum and majority approval of county is required	4	3	0	0	7
Referendum and majority approval of unincorporated area of county is required	0	0	1	0	1

TABLE 3.2
CITY-COUNTY CONSOLIDATION POTENTIAL

	Number of metro areas	Total metro population 2000	Central city percentage of metro population 2000	City-county percentage of metro population 2000	Metro governments preconsolidation	Metro governments postconsolidation
Group 0 (consolidation impossible)	58	47,625,741	25%	25%	0	0
Group 1 (consolidation improbable)	50	37,717,174	32	52	4	27
Group 2 (consolidation conceivable)	91	45,072,188	48	65	39	68
Group 3 (consolidation possible)	128	90,028,088	35	63	24	92
Totals	327	220,443,191	36	55	67	187

Note: Four central city-less metro areas (Brazoria, Tex.; Nassau-Suffolk, N.Y.; Bergen-Passaic, N.J.; and Middlesex-Somerset-Hunterdon, N.J.) are omitted.

for that matter, within the lifetimes of my grandchildren). This group includes 58 metro areas in New England, New York, New Jersey, Pennsylvania, and the District of Columbia. City-county consolidation is improbable for 50 group 1 metro areas in 5 strong, township states in the Midwest and in Virginia, where independent cities are not part of counties.[3] City-county consolidation is at least conceivable for 91 group 2 metro areas in 18 states that have weak townships or no townships at all.[4] Finally, group 3 contains 128 metro areas in 16 states where such consolidations are possible because workable state city-county consolidation laws are in place and, in 7 of the states, city-county consolidation has actually happened in recent decades.[5]

Overall, in 2000, principal central cities housed 36 percent of their regional populations in 2000. City-county consolidation would merge the land and population of unincorporated areas with the central city. The consolidated governments' share of metropolitan population would rise to 55 percent. By my definition, there were 67 metropolitan governments in 2000. City-county consolidation would raise the number to 187—over half of all metro areas. Most importantly, consolidation would give the central city effective control over most undeveloped land within the central county.

STATE ACTION TO FACILITATE CONSOLIDATION

Uniform state laws should be enacted to encourage city-county consolidation. The desirable provisions of such laws would include

1. establishing a consolidation charter commission by action of the city and county government;
2. authorizing the creation of urban and rural service districts (with different tax levels) within a consolidated government;
3. authorizing the inclusion of traditional county functions (sheriff, assessor, clerk, and so on) in the consolidated government; and
4. authorizing approval of the consolidated government by a single referendum of all affected voters (that is, no single-jurisdiction veto).

Unifying local government in metro areas is primarily a task for state government. There are too many obstacles at the local level, including entrenched officeholders, to rely on local initiative. For reforms to occur on a widespread scale, action must be taken by far-sighted and politically courageous governors and legislators.

IMPROVE ANNEXATION POWERS

In general, Table 3.1 also summarizes the relative potential of central cities in different regions to expand through annexation. While city-county consolidations are rare, municipal annexations are common. During the 1990s, of about 400 central cities that could annex, 348 did.[6] Collectively, in just one decade they expanded their municipal territory from 15,658 square miles to 18,355 square miles—about a 17 percent increase, or almost 2,700 square miles (an area slightly larger than the entire state of Delaware). Alhough most annexations occurred in the South and West, two dozen cities in strong township states did succeed in annexing land.

States should improve local annexation authority. For many small, relatively young metro areas, the central city's ability to annex urbanizing areas will be sufficient to maintain a basic unity of local government. Even in older, more built-up areas there are often opportunities for annexation that would benefit central cities. It is important to have good municipal annexation laws as tools to improve a city's elasticity. Unfortunately, during the 1990s, the trend has been in the reverse direction. In many states (notably, in Ohio, North Carolina, and Tennessee), state legislatures made annexation more difficult.

Municipal annexation is authorized by general law in forty-four states (Table 3.3). The exceptions are Hawaii and five of six New England states. Massachusetts's annexation laws (as well as those of New Jersey, New York, and Pennsylvania), however, grant only hypothetical powers since they were nullified by later statutes or by constitutional amendments.

Many states attach conditions that can severely inhibit a municipality's ability to annex. Thirty-four states allow the annexation process to be initiated by a petition of property owners in the area to be annexed. Usually the support of a majority or extraordinary majority of property owners is required. In nine of these states, annexation can be initiated only by property owner petition—a very severe limitation placing a city's expansion at the mercy of suburban developers and residents. By contrast, thirty-two states allow annexation to be initiated by city ordinance or resolution.

TABLE 3.3
STATE LAWS REGARDING MUNICIPAL ANNEXATIONS

State law	Number of states				Total USA [50]
	South [16]	West [13]	Midwest [12]	Northeast [9]	
Municipal annexation is authorized by state law	16	12	12	4	44
Initiated by property owner petition	12	10	9	3	34
Initiated by city ordinance or resolution	12	9	10	1	32
Public hearing is required	10	8	7	2	27
Referendum and majority approval in city are required	8	2	4	0	14
Referendum or majority approval in area to be annexed is required	11	3	3	2	19
Approval of county governing authority is required	1	6	4	0	11

In nineteen states a referendum or majority approval of property owners in the area to be annexed is required—another tough hurdle except where large blocs of land are owned by a handful of pro-annexation developers. In fourteen states voters in the annexing city must approve the annexation—an invitation to opposition from no-growth advocates or minority politicians fearing dilution of minority voting power.

In eleven states the affected county government must approve any municipal annexation. If the county fears loss of revenues or influence, this could be a very significant obstacle to municipal expansion.

How should the public good and private interests be balanced? I believe that state law should empower municipalities to initiate and carry out annexations while protecting property owners against unjust consequences. State statutes should protect annexed property owners against increased taxes without commensurate increased services and against unwarranted intrusion in rural lifestyles, absent significant urbanization. There should be a presumption, however, that annexation will serve the larger public interest.

In general terms, a model state annexation statute would

1. set forth the standards by which an annexation would be deemed to serve the general public interest;
2. authorize annexation to be initiated either by petition by landowners or resolution by city council;
3. require public hearings and due process;
4. authorize annexation to be consummated by council action alone; and
5. extend affected landowners the right of appeal to the state's district court in the event landowners are aggrieved because the annexation was approved or rejected in violation of state standards.

LIMIT NEW MUNICIPALITIES

The ease or difficulty with which new municipalities are formed strongly affects the degree of fragmentation of urbanizing areas into multiple local governments. Virtually all states in the South, West, and Midwest set some limitations regarding minimum population, minimum area, or minimum tax base (Table 3.4). These limitations, however, tend to be modest. With the exception of New York, northeastern states are silent on the matter. In effect, the geopolitical maps of New England, New Jersey, New York, and Pennsylvania are set in concrete. (New York's law is an anachronism since new municipalities cannot be formed.)

Sixteen states require a minimum distance between the proposed and existing municipalities. (In New Mexico, for example, the distance is five miles.) This is perhaps the most useful requirement limiting the formation of new municipalities.

Requirements regarding minimum population, minimum area, and minimum tax base should be set considerably higher than prevailing standards. State law also ought to provide for a substantial zone around existing municipalities in which the existing government can veto the incorporation of new municipalities or other public bodies, such as quasi-public water and sewer districts.

Table 3.4
State Laws Regarding Forming New Municipalities

State law	Number of states				Total USA [50]
	South [16]	West [13]	Midwest [12]	Northeast [9]	
Limits are imposed on incorporation of new local government units	15	12	12	1	40
Minimum population is required	14	12	9	1	36
Minimum area is required	5	4	7	1	17
Minimum distance from existing units is required	8	3	5	0	16
Minimum ad valorem tax base is required	0	3	3	0	6

Finally, there should be different classes of municipalities based on population size. Large cities should be given the presumptive authority over smaller cities to annex contested lands or even to absorb smaller cities in quasi-consolidation-type actions. Small municipalities, in turn, should have the right to appeal such actions to state in district court.

Create Regional Partnerships

A fourth state-based initiative is creating regional partnerships. Short of reshaping the local political map, states can authorize or mandate functional policies to achieve some of the benefits of metro governments. Forty-two states specifically authorize local governments to enter into joint powers or joint service agreements. These agreements allow local governments to band together to address problems that transcend local political boundaries. For the most part, joint powers or joint service agreements address infrastructure issues (for example, sewage treatment and air quality management) or nonthreatening service needs (for example, emergency medical services and services for senior citizens). They rarely touch the core of social and economic divisions within metro areas—housing, schools, and fiscal disparities.

There are creative exceptions, however. The Minnesota legislature mandated a multicounty tax-sharing compact for the Twin Cities area (Box 3.4). In the Portland, region, the Oregon legislature and area voters created a unique, independently elected metro government (Box 3.3) to administer infrastructure services and, most importantly, regional land use and transportation planning. The state legislatures in Massachusetts, Connecticut, and New Jersey directed suburban governments to participate in affordable housing programs (Box 3.2).

A WORD ON COUNTY GOVERNMENT

Except in the Northeast and parts of the Midwest (Box 3.6), counties have been the principal government of rural America. Counties predate urban development. They are the creation of a territorial or state legislature, which initially partitioned the territory or state's land into large governing units. As urbanization occurs, municipalities are formed to control development through planning and zoning and to provide a more intensive level of local services. Generally, county government continues to be responsible countywide (including within municipalities) for certain services—the county courts (state criminal trials), county assessor (property tax assessment), county treasurer (property tax collection), county clerk (records and elections), and often a county hospital (indigent health care). In addition, counties provide public services (typically, road and park maintenance and fire and police protection) to unincorporated areas.

County jurisdictions are remarkably stable. There are today 3,043 counties in the United States; 50 years ago there were 3,052 counties. (Such stability gave rise to the adage that "the legislature may create municipalities, but only God can create a county.")

Maryland is different, however, and I am a big fan of county government in Maryland. Even in highly urbanized areas, county government is usually the basic government. Baltimore County, for instance, covers 600 square miles, has 754,000 residents, and not a single municipality. (As an independent city separate and apart from Baltimore County, Baltimore City combines municipal and county functions.) With the nation's best mixed-income housing policies, growth management policies equal to the Portland region's, and an outstanding, countywide school system, Montgomery County, in my judgment, is the country's best urban government. And thriving downtown Bethesda (with more restaurants than downtown Louisville or uptown Charlotte) and a resurgent downtown Silver Spring show that county government can do cities with the best of city governments.

The most direct—and probably most efficient—path to creating metropolitan government in the majority of metro areas would be to empower urban county governments, have them absorb the functions and responsibilities of all municipal governments within their boundaries, and abolish all municipalities. This is an action that is fully within the legal powers of most state legislatures even if at present such sweeping urban reorganization may be beyond legislators' desires and political interests.

However, empowering county governments to provide municipal-type services outside their city limits is the worst of all possible worlds for central cities. Such state action removes all incentives for suburban land developers or future suburban residents to support municipal annexation. County government as the vehicle for regionwide unification, yes! County government as just another competitor for central cities, no!

SUMMARIZING THE STATE REGIONAL REFORM AGENDA

We have now had three decades of experience with national models illustrating best practices in the three crucial areas for regional reforms:

- To diminish racial and economic segregation and eliminate concentrated poverty, Montgomery County, Maryland's inclusionary zoning law (Box 3.1);
- To control suburban sprawl and reverse urban disinvestment, Oregon's tough State Land Use law as implemented by Portland Metro (Box 3.3); and
- To reduce fiscal imbalances that result from uneven growth and socioeconomic imbalances, Minnesota's Fiscal Disparities Plan (box 3.4).

State governments should mandate these policies both for the myriad of little boxes governments and for Big Box governments. Reformers should target governors and legislatures to adapt and adopt these successful changes in the rules of the game.

Woodrow Wilson called the states "the laboratory of democracy." America's urban problem presents states with their toughest challenge to live up to that billing.

Federal Government: Leveling the Playing Field

In any constitutional sense the federal government has no role in the way in which local governments are organized within the states. The Congress cannot, for example, mandate organization of metropolitan governments. Federal policy, nevertheless, has had a decisive impact on the emergence of suburban America since World War II and on the corresponding decline of central cities.

- The Federal Housing Administration and the Veterans Administration have backed millions of low-interest mortgages for single-family homes (largely in suburbia). By 2000 federal agencies insured or guaranteed mortgages for almost 8 million homeowners—about 20 percent of all mortgages—with an outstanding principal of $370 billion. (Federal coverage peaked at 44 percent of all home mortgages in 1956.) In addition, government-organized mortgage pools such as Fannie Mae and Freddie Mac held $2.5 trillion in mortgages in 2000.
- The Federal Highway Administration made auto-based suburbs possible. From 1956 to 2001 FHWA spent about $874 billion (in 2001 dollars) in federal aid for roads and highways (about two-thirds in urban areas). This was about six times the amount of federal aid for city-oriented mass transit ($147 billion in 2001 dollars).
- By 2003 the federal treasury will forgo over $68 billion a year in tax revenues because mortgage interest on homes (largely in the suburbs) is deductible. Another $27 billion a year in federal tax liability will be waived as a credit for state and local property taxes paid. Added to that will be over $20 billion a year as capital gains exclusions on home sales (Box 3.8). That is more than $115 billion in tax expenditures to subsidize largely suburban-oriented home own-

ership. By contrast, in 2003, federal tax law will provide only about $13 billion a year in tax credits to subsidize largely city-oriented rental housing.

Even in an era of shrinking federal aid to state and local government, federal policy continues to promote urban sprawl and the resultant decline of inelastic central cities. For fifty years national urban policy has been a national *suburban* policy.

If, as I believe, the action is really with state and local governments—and with citizens as state and local voters—what can the federal government do to encourage forming metropolitan governments? More to the point, how can the federal government reform its own policies and practices to give inelastic central cities and their poor minority residents, if not preferential advantages, then at least an even break?

FEDERAL POLICY—BACK TO THE FUTURE?

"Incentives" is a euphemism for federal money—either dollars spent or taxes not paid. Placing most central city governments on a sound financial basis, reducing racial and economic segregation, slowing urban sprawl—these are outcomes for which it would be worth considering federal incentives.

In the first edition of *Cities without Suburbs,* I proposed a series of incentives from the federal government that would reward local citizens and communities for forming metro governments. I proposed increasing the federal income tax deduction allowed for local taxes paid to metro governments, boosting the tax credit allowed for purchasing bonds issued by metro governments, and adding bonuses to grant-in-aid allocations (except Medicaid) received by metro governments.

However, when I first wrote *Cities without Suburbs* in 1992, our national debt had more than quadrupled to $4.4 trillion during the twelve years of the Reagan and Bush I administrations. Experts forecast a long-term Social Security crisis as Baby Boomers aged, but Washington chose to focus on short-term problems.

When the book's second edition appeared in 1995, the Clinton administration's 1993 tax increase and several years of budget discipline had just begun to shrink the annual federal deficit. The Social Security issue continued to fester unaddressed.

By FY 1998, with federal revenues soaring as a result of the booming economy, the federal budget embarked on an era of

---

Box 3.8 Professors Promote Homeseller Tax Reform

Surrounded by the whirring and clicking of television cameras and press photographers assembled in the Rose Garden in August 1997, the president of the United States beamed. With short strokes from a couple of dozen pens, President Clinton signed the bill that would balance the federal budget (ephemerally, as it turned out). The president handed souvenir pens to congressional leaders and administration stalwarts as mementos of the occasion.

At least one souvenir pen should have been handed out to a small band of university researchers, the Ohio Housing Research Network. They were the true authors of one important tax reform in the budget-balancing act: repeal of virtually all capital gains taxation on sales of private homes.

During 1992 researchers from seven state universities, led by Tom Bier of Cleveland State University, had poured through county court houses records. They had tracked every sale and purchase of a home in the counties surrounding Ohio's seven largest cities the previous year.

Their research yielded important insights into metropolitan housing markets. First, 81 percent of all sellers took advantage of the then-capital gains provision—that is, they rolled over any capital gain by buying a new house of equal or greater value than the house they had just sold. Of these, 84 percent moved farther out from the region's core; only 16 percent moved inward toward the city center to purchase their next home. By contrast, of the 19 per-

---

budget surpluses that would actually allow paying down the national debt. Prosperity allowed the president and Congress to project more time before the Social Security crunch would arrive.

Now, as I write *Cities without Suburbs Census 2000 Edition*, with the economy in recession, a war on terrorism to fight, and Bush II's $1.3 trillion tax cut eroding federal revenues, the prospect is red ink as far as disinterested economists can project. The Social Security crisis has come ten years closer as well (as well as my own retirement years).

The federal government clearly cannot afford to put major new money on the table for any domestic purpose except putting Social Security on a sound footing. So let me suggest how

cent who bought less expensive homes, 36 percent moved inward toward the center.

"By requiring homesellers to purchase a home priced at least equal to the one sold in order to shelter their capital gain," the Ohio researchers wrote, "the [current capital gains tax law] obstructs movement to lower-priced homes (and rental units), and it penalizes people who are forced to make such a move. In urban areas where the geographic pattern of home values is one of increasing value with distance from the center, the provision encourages movement out and away from the center, and discourages movement toward it, which exacerbates urban decline." The capital gains tax liability of homesellers should be repealed, they concluded.

It was a terrific piece of research, and I was pleased to peddle it around Washington circles. Whatever the strength of other arguments, the good politics of exempting homesellers from capital gains taxes finally took hold three years later in the midst of the presidential campaign. In August 1996 Tom Bier suddenly received a flurry of calls from White House and HUD officials asking for additional copies of the Ohio research report. President Clinton publicly launched the proposal en route to accepting the Democratic nomination in Chicago. Touted sporadically, the proposal was the closest thing to urban policy discussed in the campaign. A year later, with a $500,000 cap on the capital gain exemption for a married couple, the reform proposal had become part of the new rules of the game.

five decades of federal suburban policy can be changed to slow urban sprawl and reverse permanently the trend toward greater economic segregation (particularly of inner-city blacks and Hispanics) without spending more money.

SLOWING URBAN SPRAWL

Federal grant-in-aid programs for large public works pay a big portion of the bill for urban sprawl. Federal highway funds ($26.4 billion in FY 2001) and water system and sewage treatment grants ($3.6 billion in FY 2001) have had the greatest impact. With the federal share varying from 75 percent to 90 percent, financing major sprawl-oriented infrastructure has been virtually free for state and local governments. Let us focus on modifying how the federal government should subsidize future infrastructure projects.

Congress has already put in place regional transportation planning (Box 3.9). Congress should now put antisprawl teeth into that system. It should require Metropolitan Planning Organizations (MPOs) to analyze the impact of each project on the metropolitan area's residential density (using densities from Census 2000 as the baseline). A sliding scale for federal participation would be established for each grant-in-aid program. For example, if a proposed widening of an urban-aid highway reaching out to the metropolitan periphery would promote more sprawl and new residential development at densities 50 percent below the region's average residential density, federal participation would be reduced from 75 percent of total project costs to 25 percent. Conversely, for building a light rail line that would encourage new development at 25 percent above the region's average residential density, federal participation would increase from 75 percent to 90 percent.

Using the MPO structure, Congress should require regional planning for other federal infrastructure grants-in-aid. Oregon Congressman Earl Blumenauer (a former Portland city commissioner) advocates creating a "water ISTEA" covering federal water and sewer system grants.

The underlying principle is simple: if state and local governments want more urban sprawl, they should finance a greater portion of the costs themselves through increased state and local taxes and users fees.

REVERSING ECONOMIC SEGREGATION

There were 2,726 high-poverty census tracts where poverty rates exceeded 40 percent in the nation's metropolitan areas in 1990. Most had federal public housing projects located in or adjacent to them. Nothing in the private housing market has produced as much concentrated poverty as federal public housing policy.

In the first edition of *Cities without Suburbs*, I added my voice to the many that were calling for radical overhaul of the federal public housing program. "Housing the urban poor in high-density, inner-city public housing projects is patently destructive and should be ended as soon as possible," I wrote. "The federal court-ordered Gautreaux Project in the Chicago area has demonstrated

Box 3.9 Ice Tea: The Fed's New Regional Brew

After languishing at the federal level throughout the 1980s, regionalism was revived in 1991 when Congress passed the Intermodal Surface Transportation Efficiency Act (ISTEA). The initiative was further strengthened with the law's re-enactment as the Transportation Efficiency Act for the 21st Century (TEA-21).

Since 1973 local governments have been involved in planning the use of certain federal funds for transportation. ISTEA authorized $151 billion over six years (fiscal years 1992–7) for highway and transit assistance; TEA-21 followed with $222 billion for six years (fiscal years 1998–2003). The key change was the greater discretion afforded local officials in the use of federal funds.

In the past local planning was largely limited to prioritizing laundry lists of projects within narrow, federally prescribed program allocations. Under ISTEA/TEA-21, Metropolitan Planning Organizations (MPOs) for all urbanized areas with 200,000 or more residents have broad discretion to allocate lump-sum federal funds among road, bridge, and transit projects.

About half of all MPOs are regional councils, voluntary consortiums of local governments with a variety of program interests beyond transportation planning. Other MPOs are regional economic development organizations, transportation planning agencies, and arms of state highway departments.

In the judgment of the National Association of Regional Councils, ISTEA-TEA-21 "mark[ed] a radical and visionary transformation in the nation's transportation policy."[1]

But it is more than just about roads and rail lines. Transportation networks shape how and where people live, work, and play. Until ISTEA/TEA-21, the Federal Highway Administration and state highway departments were the masters of, not the servants of, regional land use planning.

Only the Portland and Minneapolis-St. Paul regions have regional governments combining real land use and transportation planning powers. Some regions, like Seattle-King County, have large county governments that exercise such authority.

But for most metropolitan areas, multigovernmental, designated Metropolitan Planning Organizations are the only bodies where grassroots movements can lobby for regional reforms.

1. National Association of Regional Councils, *Regional Reporter* 3 (January 1992): 1

the striking effectiveness of metrowide [rent subsidies]. . . . The federal government should adopt a Gautreaux-type strategy for public housing on a nationwide scale [see Box 3.10]."

By the turn of the millennium, a total restructuring of federal public housing policy was well under way. The federal Department of Housing and Urban Development was tearing down over 100,000 high-density, often high-rise projects and replacing them with low-density townhouses and garden apartments. Most importantly, these were mixed-income communities with as few as 25 percent of the residents being very low-income families (Box 3.11). In addition, the federal Section 8 program had expanded to subsidize rents for 2.5 million very low-income families (greatly exceeding the number of project-based apartments).

However, inner-city slums, anchored by large public housing projects, must not simply be replaced by suburban slums, filled with poor households using their vouchers to rent hand-me-down houses or cheap private apartments built for the voucher market. The goal is to assimilate low-income households into standard housing in predominantly middle-class communities. Therefore, federal regulations are essential to prevent too many poor households from reconcentrating in older suburban areas. For example, federal regulations should not allow vouchers to exceed one-third of all rental units in an apartment building or might limit vouchers to neighborhoods where the poverty rate is less than 150 percent of the area's poverty rate. (If the metro poverty rate were 10 percent, vouchers could not be used in census tracts with poverty rates of more than 15 percent.)

Does sufficient affordable housing exist in suburban areas to assimilate poor families from inner-city housing markets? Certainly a substantial amount exists; after all, most poor whites live in suburban neighborhoods. And there are a few communities that have voluntarily mandated mixed-income housing development, such as Montgomery County, Maryland (Box 3.1).

Here again, a shift in federal policy can help. After decades of fostering red-lining of inner-city neighborhoods, the federal government is redirecting private mortgage funds toward inner-city areas. The Community Reinvestment Act (CRA) requires mortgage lenders to meet new targets for mortgage and renovation loans in older neighborhoods. The federally chartered secondary mortgage market agencies like Fannie Mae and Freddie Mac must ensure that 20 percent of lending they back occurs in central cities.

Overall, such requirements have helped level the playing field. It is ironic, however, that sometimes meeting CRA goals have resulted in mortgage lenders helping build low-income housing projects precisely where they should not be built: in already poverty-impacted, inner-city neighborhoods. The CRA and other federal regulations should be amended to allow mixed-income housing in suburban areas, accessible to former public housing tenants, to meet federal goals as well.

Moreover, Fannie Mae and Freddie Mac sponsor many special mortgage programs to achieve different social goals, such as encouraging more minority homeownership or helping first-time buyers. They should adopt a new policy to reward communities for implementing inclusionary zoning policies. All homeowners in an inclusionary neighborhood should be eligible for lower-interest loans (say, one point below prevailing market). To qualify, an inclusionary neighborhood would have to meet two tests: 1) having at least 15 or 20 percent affordable housing, and 2) having a regional public housing agency acquire one-third of the affordable units.

The greatest fear (at least, expressed fear) of homeowners to the mixed-income concept is that having lower-income neighbors would reduce the value of their market-rate homes. In the context of a Montgomery County-type policy, that fear is ungrounded (Box 3.1). However, providing lower-interest mortgages to all homeowners would convert that economic fear into an undeniable economic benefit in the form of lower mortgage payments for everyone in the neighborhood.

This proposed federal regional reform agenda is based on two principles. First, echoing the old Hippocratic oath, "do no more harm." Second, reflecting the ups and downs of the federal fiscal and budgetary teeter-totter, "spend no more money." If the federal government truly reformed the way it does business in urban America as outlined above, state and local governments might be motivated to change substantially the way they approach metropolitan development issues—the rules of the game.

Building Grassroots Coalitions

What will motivate state and local governments to change their ways are politically powerful grassroots reform movements. As I stated in the preface, "what this decade has taught me most is

**Box 3.10 From Failure in the Ghetto
to Success in the Suburbs**

The Gautreaux Project proved that public housing tenants in inner cities can succeed simply by getting out of bad neighborhoods
into better neighborhoods. The project was named for public-
housing tenant activist Dorothy Gautreaux, lead plaintiff in a suit
brought in 1976 in which the federal courts found the Chicago
Housing Authority (CHA) guilty of racial discrimination. One
remedy the courts ordered was to subsidize moving public housing families out of CHA projects and into private rental housing
elsewhere in Chicago or anywhere in Chicago's six-county suburban area.

Between 1981 and 1998 over 7,100 families participated in the
program, administered by the Leadership Council for Metropolitan Open Communities, a court-appointed nonprofit organization. One-third of the families remained in Chicago; two-thirds
moved to Chicago's suburbs.

James E. Rosenbaum, professor of sociology at Northwestern
University, did a follow-up study of the "city stayers" and "suburban movers."[1] Both showed the same socioeconomic profile entering the program: typically a black, female head of household,
receiving welfare assistance, with two or three children. Of the
suburban-mover mothers, 64 percent were working compared
with 51 percent for city-stayer mothers. Of the suburban-mover
children, 95 percent graduated from their suburban systems compared with a graduation rate of 80 percent of city stayers from
Chicago schools. Fifty-four percent of suburban movers had continued their education (27 percent in four-year colleges) com-

that building political coalitions to achieve fundamental reforms
in the 'rules of the game' is hard, time-consuming work."

Over the past decade I have worked with many different individuals and organizations in over 100 metropolitan areas. To
reach critical mass politically in order to bring about fundamental reforms, many different interest groups must come together.
Partners in such coalitions should include

- environmental groups, such as Louisville's River Fields,
New Jersey Future, and 1,000 Friends of Wisconsin, who
recognize that Smart Growth must also be Fair Growth, ad-
vancing social equity as well as protecting the environment;

pared with 21 percent of city stayers (4 percent in four-year colleges). Seventy-five percent of suburban-mover youth were working (21 percent for hourly wages of $6.50 or better); by contrast, only 41 percent of city-stayer youth had a job (5 percent at $6.50 or better per hour).[2]

"Pessimistic predictions of 'culture of poverty' models are not supported," Rosenbaum concluded after completing his study. "The early experiences of low-income blacks do not prevent them from benefiting from suburban moves."

One participant in the Gautreaux Project summed up her experience: "A housing project deteriorates you. You don't want to do anything. Living in the suburbs made me feel that I'm worth something. I can do anything I want to do if I get up and try it."

The Gautreaux Project had a major impact on federal housing assistance policies, turning HUD away from concentrating poor families in large projects toward integrating them in mixed-income communities through rent vouchers used on a regionwide basis and tearing down large projects and rebuilding them as mixed-income neighborhoods under HOPE VI grants.

1. James E. Rosenbaum, "Black Pioneers—Do Their Moves to the Suburbs Increase Economic Opportunity for Mothers and Children?" in Federal National Mortgage Association (Fannie Mae), *Housing Policy Debate* 2: 1213.
2. Outcomes for both suburban movers and city stayers were presumably superior to those for households remaining in many of Chicago's high-rise public housing projects.

- affordable housing advocates, such as Trenton's ISLES, Florida Housing Coalition, and Massachusetts Housing Partnership, who know that success means not just providing low-income families with affordable shelter but with access to mainstream opportunity;
- civil rights organizations, such as the Urban League and Chicago's Leadership Council for Metropolitan Open Communities (Box 3.10), who understand that exclusionary zoning is now the preferred instrument of social segregation;
- farmland preservation groups, such as the Michigan Farm Bureau, whose president Jack Laurie memorably stated "To save our farms, we must save our cities";

Box 3.11 Big Business Targets Chicago Regional Reforms

We have created an increasingly polarized society. The poor live mainly in the central city and inner suburbs, while the more affluent live chiefly in the central core of the region and in the outer suburbs. When a substantial minority of the population is shut out, isolated, and without hope, the economic and social well-being of the whole region is threatened.

The fate of everyone in this region is inherently connected. There is a common interest, a common good, and it cuts across municipal boundaries and binds us into one metropolitan community. In this era of unprecedented prosperity, we would be a hollow and near-sighted people indeed if we were to neglect issues concerning human dignity and equality of opportunity, community and environmental integrity, and the ideals and civilizing purposes of a great metropolitan region.

The report created a major stir both for what it said and for who said it—the Commercial Club of Chicago, an organization of 400 of the Chicago region's most important business leaders. Almost a century earlier, the Commercial Club had commissioned the sweeping *Plan of Chicago* by Daniel H. Burnham that had shaped the growth of Chicago's world-class Loop and lakefront.

Now with this report, *Chicago Metropolis 2020*, the Commercial Club had undertaken an even more daunting task—reversing the impact of suburban sprawl, racial segregation, and economic isolation that threatened the vitality of Greater Chicago.

- regional planning bodies, such as Peoria's Tri-County Planning Commission, Kansas City's Mid-America Regional Council, the Atlanta Regional Council, the Association of Central Oklahoma Governments, and St. Louis's East-West Gateway Coordinating Council that are willing to push the envelope for regional reforms;
- labor unions, who have grasped as a result of analysis by the AFL-CIO's Good Jobs First program that urban sprawl places jobs beyond unions' reach;
- urban studies centers such as University of Minnesota's Institute on Race and Poverty, University of New Orleans's College of Urban Planning, and the Ohio Urban Universities Program (Box 3.8), that are sources of research, strategy, and student and faculty manpower; and

To implement its plan (drafted by Elmer W. Johnson, now president of the Aspen Institute), in March 1999 the Commercial Club organized a new, nonprofit group, Chicago Metropolis 2020 (<www.chicagometropolis2020.org>), with a blue-ribbon, fifty-member board of top business, labor, and civic leaders and two prominent, former steel industry executives, George A. Ranney, Jr., and Frank H. Beal, as president/CEO and executive director.

The group's first victory was leading a coalition of organizations in securing the state legislature's approval of the $12 billion Illinois First infrastructure package. A much less conventional step, however, was the group's championing of the Metropolis Principles. Over 100 major area employers pledged that "in making decisions relating to the expansion of an existing facility or the location of a new facility in a given community, we will give substantial weight to whether a community has zoning, building, and land use policies that allow the construction of housing which is affordable to working people; and whether a community is served by reliable and accessible mass transit, especially mass transit near work sites." Signatories included such giants as American Airlines, Bank of America, BP Amoco, Citibank, McDonald's Corporation, Motorola, Sears, Roebuck and Co., Tribune Publishing Company, and United Airlines.

Chicago Metropolis 2020's ambitious agenda includes sweeping reforms in public education and child care, transportation, land use and housing policy, workforce development, municipal finance, and regional governance.

- central city governments and coalitions of older, declining suburbs (Box 3.5) that are increasingly united against a common foe—urban sprawl.

However, there are two essential players—business organizations and interfaith coalitions. Respected business groups such as the Greater Baltimore Committee, Silicon Valley Manufacturers Group, Better York, Chicago Metropolis 2020 (Box 3.11), and the Allegheny Conference on Community Development bring access, influence, credibility, and resources to the regional reform movement.

But the business groups cannot mobilize large numbers of people. For that we must look to the rise of a network of faith-based coalitions committed to changing the rules of the game

---

Box 3.12. Faith-Based Coalitions Champion Fair Growth

Cancellation of Chicago's sprawl-generating South Suburban Expressway into southern Lake County, Indiana . . . shifting future alignment of commuter rail from serving subdivisions planned for south county farmlands to serving Gary and Hammond's first-ring suburbs . . . lobbying successfully for a state law authorizing a regional transit agency, supported by a new, earmarked tax, that will carry city residents to suburban jobs . . . successfully challenging the federal government's recertification of the Metropolitan Planning Organization . . . all this in addition to closing inner-city crack houses and successfully opposing a new county landfill on the edge of city neighborhoods—what's going on in Chicago's suburbs in northwest Indiana?

What is happening is the Interfaith Federation of Northwest Indiana, a remarkable grassroots coalition of over forty congregations—Protestant, Catholic, Jewish, Muslim; blacks, whites, Hispanics—organizing their central cities (Gary, Hammond, East Chicago) and older suburbs (Merrillville, Griffith, Hobart).

The Interfaith Federation is just one of four dozen interfaith coalitions affiliated with the Gamaliel Foundation based in Chicago. Detroit's MOSES, Cleveland's NOAH, Metropolitan Congregations United for St. Louis, Baltimore BRIDGE, the Twin Cities' Isaiah Project, Chicago's Metropolitan Alliance of Congregations, Saginaw's Ezekiel, Buffalo's VOICE, and dozens more are driving forces for the American Metropolitan Equities Network

---

through metropolitan- and state-level action (Box 3.12). Affiliated with the Chicago-based Gamaliel Foundation, faith communities are organizing across denominational lines, across racial, ethnic and class divides, across city, town, and township boundaries for political action. Their targets are city halls, county courthouses, and state capitols.

When committed citizens pour out of the church buses by the hundreds and even thousands to pack public hearings and legislative galleries, politicians listen . . . and act. The future of metropolitan America will be determined not in the corridors of power but in the pulpits and pews where determined leaders—clerical and lay—are mobilizing the "angels of our better nature."

(AMEN) agenda. Organizing across denominational, racial and ethnic, and jurisdictional lines, the Gamaliel network (<http://www.gamaliel.org>) has made changing the rules of the game in order to achieve social justice its core goal. They have become powerful advocates of regional, antisprawl land use and transportation planning, regional fair share mixed-income housing, and regional tax-base sharing.

Such faith-based coalitions are the vanguard of the new civil rights movement. They magnify their moral outrage against growing social disparities through the ability to mobilize large numbers of people.

Another demonstration. Determined to abandon the federal courthouse in downtown Hammond to build a new courthouse twenty-five miles away in Crown Point, senior federal district court judges had already secured Congress's blessing, the General Services Administration's approval, all necessary federal appropriations, and a new site. It was a done deal.

Unwilling to see the city lose key jobs, the Interfaith Federation stopped the move. The new federal courthouse was built in downtown Hammond.

In American society nobody believes themselves more sovereign than federal judges. The Interfaith Federation beat them at their own game on their own turf.

That's people power.

Notes

1. I am indebted to John P. Blair of Wright State University for coining the phrase "elasticity mimics."

2. No smaller municipality ever appears to have joined voluntarily into the larger, consolidated entity. Of the major postwar consolidations, there are seven municipal enclaves in Nashville-Davidson, fifteen (three cities and twelve towns) in Indianapolis-Marion, four in Jacksonville-Duval, one in Columbus-Muskogee, two in Athens-Clarke, two in Augusta-Richmond, and ninety-three in Louisville-Jefferson. Fayette County seems to have contained no other municipality when it merged with Lexington.

3. The group 1 strong "township states" (all part of the old Northwest territories) are Illinois, Michigan, Minnesota, Ohio, and Wisconsin. In Virginia, there were technically a half dozen city-county consolidations, like Virginia-Beach-

Princess Anne County. However, all were really maneuvers to municipalize suburban counties to prevent further annexations by Norfolk, Portsmouth, and Newport News.

4. Group 2 states are Alabama, Arizona, Arkansas, Delaware, Idaho, Iowa, Kansas, Maryland, Mississippi, Missouri, Nebraska, Nevada, North Dakota, Oklahoma, South Dakota, Texas, West Virginia, and Wyoming. All have weak townships or are considered so-called county states.

5. Group 3 states are California, Colorado, Louisiana, New Mexico, North Carolina, Oregon, South Carolina, Utah, and Washington, and Alaska, Florida, Georgia, Hawaii, Indiana, Kentucky, Montana, and Tennessee, where postwar consolidations have occurred. All are county states except Indiana, whose townships are weak.

6. Central cities that could not annex land included ninety-five in New England, New York, New Jersey, and Pennsylvania; Virginia's fifteen larger independent cities; and about two dozen older central cities (e.g., Cleveland, Detroit, and Chicago) that were completely surrounded by incorporated suburbs or were already consolidated city-counties (e.g., Baltimore, Denver, New Orleans, Philadelphia, San Francisco, and St, Louis as well as more recent consolidations mentioned).

Chapter IV

Conclusions

"You may have shifted from a theme of cities without suburbs to suburbs with incidental cities," commented my colleague Hank Savitch in 1992 after reviewing an early draft of the first edition of this book.

> Your central argument is that cities "succeed" only if they continue to absorb suburbs, which you see as America's preferred lifestyle. City survival ought not be so dependent upon imitating suburban patterns. How can cities become viable again within a metropolitan environment? Frankly, I believe that cities do have different roles to play.

His comments brought me up short. I love old-fashioned, bustling downtowns, and I love the old apartment buildings and town houses, nearby shops, tree-lined streets, mini-parks, buses, and subways of good urban neighborhoods. There is nothing sadder than a city that undertakes a redevelopment project that looks and functions like a suburban office park and shopping mall.

As mayor I often spoke of Albuquerque as "a giant suburb in search of a city." Albuquerque had all the suburban lifestyle its advocates could possibly want, I suggested. Albuquerque needed to strengthen its urban character. With modest success and much controversy, I promoted downtown Albuquerque as a center of business, government, entertainment, and the arts.

Having returned to Washington, D.C., in 1991, we live again in the District of Columbia in a condominium twelve minutes from the White House. At our front door is a Metro bus stop; at our back door, a two-mile long ribbon of wooded trails. Three food markets, two pharmacies, two toy stores, a book store, barber shops and beauty salons, dry cleaners, a florist, two banks, four restaurants, two Starbucks, and a dozen other stores lie within a ten-minute walk.

The choice that my wife, Delcia, and I made to live in the city when we returned to the Washington area was not unusual. During the 1990s tens of thousands of empty nesters like us moved back to many cities around the country. The demographic impact of returning empty nesters was certainly exceeded by the hundreds of thousands of young professionals—singles, "mingles," young marrieds without children, gay couples—that opted for the diversity, excitement, cultural richness, and convenience of big city living. The core areas of Washington, Baltimore, Cleveland, Philadelphia, Portland, and several dozen older cities began to thrive with an urban vitality that in previous decades seemed to have been preserved only by New York, Chicago, Boston, Seattle, and San Francisco. Many downtowns and surrounding historic neighborhoods, beefed up with new condos and townhouses, became virtual yuppie theme parks. Certainly, this was one of the "different roles" that cities could play that Hank Savitch alluded to.

Another "different role" was a traditional function that many cities recovered in the past decade—the doorway to a new life for millions of immigrants. A cherished chapter of our national legend (at least, in retrospect) is how millions of European immigrants—Germans, Irish, Italians, Greeks, Poles, and other Eastern Europeans—first touched our shores at Ellis Island, then fanned out into their new country's cities to man the factories of the world's emerging industrial power.

That historic flow of immigrants was largely suspended from the early 1920s through the mid-1960s, in part, because of the Great Depression, World War II, the Cold War, and Europe's economic revival. Most importantly, however, the Congress enacted a very restrictive immigration law in 1923 that established quotas based on the national origins of the American population as of the 1920 census. This effectively slammed the door in the face of most would-be immigrants who were from Asia, Latin America, and Africa. (Fifteen million African Americans, whose ancestors were brought to America as slaves, were not accorded the dignity of a "national origin.") Only in 1965 did the Congress liberalize America's immigration laws again.

Thus, for the first two postwar decades, many older cities (which were often inelastic cities as well) were confronted by three simultaneous demographic trends: white, middle-class families moving to the burgeoning new suburbs; rural blacks moving from southern farms into cities South and North; and a relative trickle of immigrants arriving from abroad. For inelastic central cities, it was a formula for steady decline in total population combined with rapid increase in the proportion of African Americans.

During the 1990s, however, swelling immigration lifted the United States to its highest rate of population growth since the postwar baby boom. Census 2000 also recorded the highest percentage of foreign-born residents since 1910. Massive immigration reversed the population decline of some inelastic cities. For example, of the 119 principal central cities studied in chapter II, there were 18 inelastic cities that could not annex new land but still saw population increases during the 1990s. Hispanic immigration accounted totally for the net population increases in 13 of the 18 cities, including Chicago, Boston, Providence, and Minneapolis. Hispanic and Asian immigration combined accounted completely for New York City's reaching a record 8 million residents. Of all central cities with now-fixed city limits, only Atlanta, Denver, Seattle, and San Francisco added white residents.

Yet the few thousands of new white residents of Atlanta, Denver, Seattle, and San Francisco added zero children to their cities' public schools. They either had no children or sent them to private schools.

In fact, across metropolitan America, the melting pot of our public school systems was developing cracks. Segregation of black pupils continued to diminish slowly except where an increasingly conservative federal judiciary dismantled long-standing school desegregation orders. (Returning black children to their neighborhood schools meant sending them back to racially segregated schools.) Segregation of Hispanic and Asian pupils, however, grew wherever a major influx of new immigrants occurred. In most regions, economic segregation—the separation of low-income pupils from middle-class pupils—increased.

Why is this important? The principal reason is that by far the two most important predictors of academic success or failure are the income and educational attainment of a child's parents, and the same factors for a child's classmates. The socioeconomic status of the kids in the classroom is much more important than expenditures per pupil, class size, teacher experience, instructional materials, or competition from charter or private schools that are

the typical focus of school reformers. As sociologist James Coleman wrote in his landmark *Equality of Educational Opportunity*
(1966), "The educational resources provided by a child's fellow
students are more important for his achievement than are the resources provided by the school board." So important are fellow
students, Coleman found, that "the social composition of the student body is more highly related to achievement, independent of
the student's own social background, than is any school factor."[1]

Summarizing the enormous body of research, the Century
Foundation's Richard D. Kahlenberg writes

> What makes a school good or bad is not so much the physical
> plant and facilities as the people involved in it—the students, the
> parents, and the teachers. The portrait of the nation's high poverty
> schools is not just a racist or classist stereotype: high-poverty
> schools are often marked by students who have less motivation
> and are often subject to negative peer influences; parents who are
> generally less active, exert less clout in school affairs, and garner
> fewer financial resources for the school; and teachers who tend to
> be less qualified, to have lower expectations, and to teach a wa-
> tered-down curriculum. Giving all students access to schools with
> a core of middle-class students and parents will significantly raise
> the overall quality of schooling in America.

Coleman's study and of scores of others can be summarized in
three findings. Finding 1: Socioeconomic status of pupils and
classmates largely determines academic outcomes. Finding 2:
Poor children learn best surrounded by middle-class classmates.
Finding 3: Middle-class pupils do just fine whether they have 5
percent or 25 percent low-income classmates.

In recent years, these findings have been consistently—I
would say even deliberately—ignored by almost all politicians
and many educators. They refuse to discuss (much less deal
with) the racial and class substructure of American society because too many benefit from maintaining such divisions. Yet
economic integration works. Mixing poor children into predominantly middle-class classrooms would be the most effective way
to raise performance levels.

This is why, in my view, there is something unsettling about
the nature of the rebound of a number of inelastic cities in the
1990s. We are creating enclave cities where islands of higher-in-
come, childless, largely white professional households are sealed

off from declining neighborhoods of ever poorer, mostly minority families. Meanwhile, many black and Hispanic middle-class families are themselves moving to closer-in suburbs only to find that many young, white middle-class families have already decamped to the outer suburbs, taking better jobs, better shopping, and the best schools with them.

As Mayor William Johnson of Rochester, New York, reflecting on his decades as an Urban League executive, said, "We prepared ourselves for opportunity without realizing that opportunity was being relentlessly relocated beyond our reach."

Twenty-five years ago I raised these themes—suburban sprawl, urban disinvestment, racial, ethnic, and economic segregation, all compounded by jurisdictional fragmentation—at the U.S. Conference of Mayors. I got virtually no support. Suburban mayors did not want to think about central cities. They believed their constituents had said goodbye and good riddance to the city. Central city mayors—more and more, black or Hispanic—did not want to hear any proposals that might threaten their political comfort levels. After all, black and Hispanic communities had worked long and hard to get real power at city hall.

City and suburban mayors alike were unwilling to attack the urban problem as a matter of racial and economic segregation. From the suburban perspective, the strategy was to quarantine "them" in inner-city ghettos and barrios away from "us" and (maybe) help "them" rebuild from within with more federal and state money. For many central city mayors, "them" was "us"— the political base of their power. "Just `empower' us," they said, "and we'll do the job of fighting urban poverty." ("Empower" typically meant "send more federal and state money.") Both suburban and city officials implicitly believed that separate could be made equal, or at least equal enough to be tolerable.

"Separate but equal" cannot work. It has never worked. Ghettos and barrios create and perpetuate an urban underclass. Bad communities defeat good programs. Successful clients of social programs typically move away. In inner cities, individual success rarely translates into community success. Life in ghettos and barrios gets worse. Despite flourishing downtowns, most inner-city neighborhoods deteriorate as places to raise families. With shrinking tax bases, city budgets are unable to meet rising social needs.

Enterprise zones, community development banks, nonprofit inner-city housing developers—all tools of empowerment—are not futile efforts. They produce some new businesses, some new jobs, some new homes, and some revitalized neighborhoods. They are more effective, however, if carried out within a framework of actions to bring down the walls between city and suburb.

National urban policy, state-by-state urban policy, and area-by-area urban policy must focus on breaking up ghettos and barrios. Urban policy must systematically help ghetto and barrio residents become integrated into the entire metropolitan area. It is the very isolation and hyperconcentration of poor minorities that overwhelms them individually. Neither poor people nor inner cities can succeed if they are cast into the sociological equivalents of giant public housing projects.

Throughout history cities have been the arena of opportunity and upward mobility. In America the "city" has been redefined since World War II. The real city is now the whole urban area—city and suburb—the metropolitan area. Redeeming inner cities and the urban underclass requires reintegration of city and suburb.

This is the toughest political issue in American society. It goes right to the heart of Americans' fears about race and class. There will be no short-term, politically comfortable solutions.

How metro areas are organized has greatly affected the degree of racial and economic segregation. Within their expanding municipal boundaries, elastic, Big Box cities capture much suburban-style growth. As the urban core expands, much wealth still remains within the Big Box; elastic cities minimize city-suburb disparities. In addition, neighborhood-by-neighborhood, different racial, ethnic, and economic groups mix together more readily within a Big Box than they do among many little boxes. Little boxes regions function to divide rather than unify.

How can responsibility for poor minorities be made a metropolitanwide responsibility? How can all jurisdictions—city and suburb—assume their fair share?

Traditionally, the primary purpose of regional cooperation among local governments has been the delivery of public services. Regional arrangements usually avoid policies and programs that share the social burdens of inner-city residents. Yet this is the heart of the challenge. Area-wide compacts on transportation planning, solid-waste management, sewage treatment, and air quality management may be good government, but they do not address the urban problem—racial and economic segregation.

For many small and medium-size metro areas, the best framework for reversing patterns of racial and economic segregation is to create metro governments. This can be achieved by expanding the central city through aggressive annexation policies, by consolidating the city and county, or by fully empowering county government and abolishing or reducing the role of municipalities in key regional issues such as land use and transportation planning, mixed-income housing policy, and economic development.

For larger, more complex metro areas, metro government may be neither politically feasible nor administratively desirable for delivering services. Larger government is not necessarily more efficient government. At any scale, efficiency is largely a function of good management. Given the bureaucratic impulse of many large systems, a metro government may be less efficient and less responsive as a deliverer of services than smaller governments.

It is not important that local residents have their garbage picked up by a metrowide garbage service or their parks managed by a metrowide parks and recreation department. It is important that all local governments pursue common policies that will diminish racial and economic segregation. The following three policies are essential:

- To diminish racial and economic segregation and eliminate concentrated poverty, implement regional inclusionary zoning and other mixed-income housing strategies for integrating low-income households into middle-class communities;
- To control suburban sprawl and reverse urban disinvestment, implement regional land use and transportation planning and growth management strategies; and
- To reduce fiscal imbalances that result from uneven growth and socioeconomic imbalances, implement regional tax base sharing between richer and poorer jurisdictions.

State government must play the leading role. Local government is the creature of state government. State government sets the ground rules for how local governments are organized and what they are empowered to do. Furthermore, governors and state legislators can and do act as metrowide policymakers. State government also plays an increasingly important role in financing local government (especially, public schools). With the purse comes additional power and responsibility to make the organization of metro areas more rational and equitable.

State government must act in two directions. First, build metropolitan institutions by

- improving annexation laws to facilitate continuous central city expansion into urbanizing areas;
- enacting laws to encourage city-county consolidation or mandating consolidation by direct statute; and
- empowering county government in highly balkanized, little boxes states so that they can act as metro governments in key policy and service areas.

Second, setting new rules of the game by

- requiring all local governments in metro areas to provide fair share affordable housing, including adopting local inclusionary zoning ordinances;
- enacting strong, antisprawl, statewide growth management laws; and
- establishing metrowide tax base sharing arrangements or utilizing state aid to help equalize local revenues.

As I stated earlier, reorganizing local government is primarily a state and local task. There are key roles, however, for the federal government. Since World War II the federal government's urban policy has been suburban policy. It is past time for the federal government to deal with the consequences of its handiwork through penalizing rather than rewarding sprawl through its infrastructure grants, strengthening the scope of metropolitan planning organizations, and promoting mixed-income housing through its various housing finance mechanisms.

Over 80 percent of all minorities now live in America's metropolitan areas. A racially equitable society can be achieved only if urban America is changed. Conversely, solving the problems of cities requires addressing the city-suburb schisms that have intensified since World War II.

More than increased urban aid or even a true urban policy, what is most needed is a commitment to a spirit of shared sacrifice and renewal. We must exchange the old politics of exclusion for a new politics of inclusion. Solving our urban problem will test whether or not the American people can develop a new

spirit of community. Can we truly become *E Pluribus Unum*—
from the many, one?

Notes

1. Quoted in Richard D. Kahlenberg, *All Together Now: Creating Middle-Class Schools through Public School Choice* (Washington, D.C.: Brookings Institution Press, 2001), 28; subsequent quote on page 47. Kahlenberg's thirty-three pages of footnotes to chapters 3 and 4 catalog most of the major studies that have been done on the effects of racial and economic integration of public schools.

Appendix

Central Cities and Metro Areas by Elasticity Category

The appendix ranks 521 central cities by their relative elasticity within the different categories outlined in chapter II for metropolitan areas. (Another 20 central cities are not ranked because data were not available for 1950, often because the cities did not exist at that date.) Both central cities and metropolitan areas are listed as defined for Census 2000. The cities are ranked in ascending order of elasticity. The most inelastic city is ranked first in the zero elasticity column. The most elastic city will be listed last in the hyper elasticity column.

These rankings are more art than exact science. Cities with sharply different circumstances can sometimes have the same elasticity score. When cities have the same score, I have ranked the city with the higher initial density in 1950 as the more inelastic. Readers should not get caught up in slight differences in elasticity rankings but focus where each city falls among the broad categories.

In each table a city that is in uppercase letters (for example, OAKLAND, Calif.) is considered to be the primary or historic central city for that metro area (MSA or PMSA). A city in lowercase (for example, Berkeley, Calif.) is considered to be a secondary central city. In instances where two or more central cities are designated in the metro area's title, I have chosen the first named. Thus, MINNEAPOLIS, Minn., is the primary central city, and St. Paul, Minn., is the secondary central city.

An asterisk (*) following a city's name indicates that the city was already considered a central city in the 1950 census.

139

TABLE A-1
161 CENTRAL CITIES OVER 100,000 POPULATION PRIMARILY IN LARGE METRO AREAS (MORE THAN 250,000)

27 zero elastic cities	Elasticity score	31 low elastic cities	Elasticity score	39 medium elastic cities	Elasticity score	31 high Elastic cities	Elasticity score	33 hyper elastic cities	Elasticity score
NEW YORK, N.Y.*	4.0	CHICAGO, Ill.*	11.5	PEORIA, Ill.*	19.5	KNOXVILLE, Tenn.*	26.5	LITTLE ROCK, Ark.*	31.0
NEWARK, N.J.*	4.0	OAKLAND, Calif.*	11.5	ANN ARBOR, Mich.	19.5	_WICHITA FALLS, Tex.*_	26.5	Winston-Salem, N.C.	31.0
BOSTON, Mass.*	4.0	ALLENTOWN, Pa.*	11.5	DES MOINES, Iowa*	19.5	MODESTO, Calif.	26.5	ALBUQUERQUE, N.M.*	31.0
DETROIT, Mich.*	4.0	CINCINNATI, Ohio*	11.5	Santa Ana, Calif.	20.0	SANTA ROSA, Calif.	26.5	Escondido, Calif.	31.0
WASHINGTON, D.C.*	4.0	Portsmouth, Va.	12.0	ROCKFORD, Ill.*	20.5	SHREVEPORT, La.*	27.0	LAS VEGAS, Nev.	31.0
HARTFORD, Conn.*	5.0	ERIE, Pa.*	13.0	FORT LAUDERDALE, Fla.	20.5	LAFAYETTE, La	27.0	HUNTSVILLE, Ala.	31.0
ROCHESTER, N.Y.*	5.0	SEATTLE, Wash.*	13.0	SALINAS, Calif.	20.5	_WACO, Tex.*_	27.0	SAN DIEGO, Calif.*	31.5
Cambridge, Mass.	5.5	STAMFORD, Conn.*	13.0	VENTURA, Calif.	21.0	WICHITA, Kans.*	27.5	LEXINGTON, Ky.*	32.0
ST LOUIS, Mo.*	5.5	Hampton, Va.	13.0	PORTLAND, Ore.*	21.5	_SIOUX FALLS, S.D.*_	27.5	SAN ANTONIO, Tex.*	32.0
PROVIDENCE, R.I.*	5.5	Arlington, Va.	13.5	Joliet, Ill.	22.0	Kansas City, Kans.	28.0	_LUBBOCK, Tex._	32.0
SYRACUSE, N.Y.*	6.0	NEW ORLEANS, La.*	13.5	Clearwater, Fla.	22.0	TAMPA, Fla.*	28.0	MONTGOMERY, Ala.*	32.0
MINNEAPOLIS, Minn.*	6.5	LOUISVILLE, Ky.*	14.0	ANAHEIM, Calif.	22.0	Irving, Tex.	28.0	HOUSTON, Tex.*	32.0
SAN FRANCISCO, Calif.*	7.0	Waterbury, Conn.*	14.0	Tempe, Ariz.	22.0	Durham, N.C.*	28.5	COLUMBUS, Ga.*	32.5
BUFFALO, N.Y.*	7.0	Long Beach, Calif.	14.5	SAVANNAH, Ga.*	22.5	MOBILE, Ala.*	28.5	NASHVILLE, Tenn.*	33.0
PITTSBURGH, Pa.*	8.0	Pasadena, Calif.	14.5	_SPRINGFIELD, Ill.*_	22.5	JACKSON, Miss.*	28.5	AUGUSTA, Ga.*	33.0
CLEVELAND, Ohio*	8.0	GRAND RAPIDS, Mich.*	15.0	ATLANTA, Ga.*	23.0	MEMPHIS, Tenn.*	29.0	SAN JOSE, Calif.*	33.0
BALTIMORE, Md.*	8.0	FLINT, Mich.*	15.0	DENVER, Colo.*	23.0	TULSA, Okla.*	29.5	_ABILENE, Tex._	33.0
NEW HAVEN, Conn.*	8.0	AKRON, Ohio*	15.0	OMAHA, Nebr.*	23.0	COLUMBIA, S.C.*	29.5	CORPUS CHRISTI, Tex.*	33.0

City	Score
St. Paul, Minn.*	8.0
JERSEY CITY, N.J.*	8.5
PHILADELPHIA, Pa.*	8.5
WORCESTER, Mass.*	9.0
SPRINGFIELD, Mass.*	9.0
Berkeley, Calif.	9.5
BRIDGEPORT, Conn.*	9.5
MIAMI, Fla.*	10.0
LOWELL, Mass.*	10.5
TACOMA, Wash.*	15.0
MANCHESTER, N.H.*	15.0
LOS ANGELES, Calif.*	15.5
MILWAUKEE, Wisc.*	16.0
TOLEDO, Ohio*	16.5
NORFOLK, Va.*	16.5
DAYTON, Ohio*	17.0
RICHMOND, Va.*	17.0
SOUTH BEND, Ind.*	17.0
EVANSVILLE, Ind.*	17.5
GARY, Ind.	18.0
St. Petersburg, Fla.	18.0
LANSING, Mich.*	18.5
PUEBLO, Colo.*	23.0
FORT WAYNE, Ind.*	23.5
Aurora, Ill.	23.5
VALLEJO, Calif.	23.5
RIVERSIDE, Calif.	23.5
San Bernardino, Calif.*	24.0
CEDAR RAPIDS, Iowa*	24.0
TOPEKA, Kans.*	24.5
MADISON, Wisc.*	24.5
STOCKTON, Calif.*	24.5
BATON ROUGE, La.*	24.5
GREEN BAY, Wisc.	24.5
BIRMINGHAM, Ala.*	25.0
Vancouver, Wash.	25.0
SACRAMENTO, Calif.*	25.5
SALEM, Ore.	25.5
Sunnyvale, Calif.	25.5
BEAUMONT, Tex.*	25.5
Newport News, Va.	26.0
COLUMBUS, Ohio*	26.0
LINCOLN, Nebr.*	26.0
CHATTANOOGA, Tenn.*	29.5
RENO, Nev.	29.5
Arlington, Tex.	29.5
INDIANAPOLIS, Ind.*	30.0
KANSAS CITY, Mo.*	30.0
FAYETTEVILLE, N.C.	30.0
AMARILLO, Tex.	30.0
FORT WORTH, Tex.*	30.0
FRESNO, Calif.*	30.5
RALEIGH, N.C.*	30.5
GREENSBORO, N.C.*	30.5
DALLAS, Tex.*	30.5
ORLANDO, Fla.*	30.5
JACKSONVILLE, Fla.*	34.0
BAKERSFIELD, Calif.	34.0
CHARLOTTE, N.C.*	34.0
PHOENIX, Ariz.*	35.0
TALLAHASSEE, Fla.	35.0
AUSTIN, Tex.*	35.0
COLORADO SPRINGS, Colo.	35.5
TUCSON, Ariz.	35.5
CLARKSVILLE, Tenn.	35.5
Mesa, Ariz.	35.5
ATHENS, Ga.	35.5
OKLAHOMA CITY, Okla.*	36.0
Scottsdale, Ariz.	37.0
Virginia Beach, Va.	38.5
ANCHORAGE, Alaska	40.0

Notes: A city in uppercase letters is considered to be the primary or historic central city for that metro area. A city in lowercase letters is considered to be a secondary city. Asterisk (*) indicates that city was designated as central city in 1950; italics indicate that metro population was less than 250,000 in 2000; central cities over 100,000 not evaluated because of lack of 1950 data (generally, not yet incorporated): Bellevue, Wash., Cape Coral, Fla., and Irvine and Lancaster, Calif.

Table A-2
191 Central Cities under 100,000 Population in Large Metro Areas (More than 250,000)

40 zero elastic cities	Elasticity score	37 low elastic cities	Elasticity score	38 medium elastic cities	Elasticity score	40 high Elastic cities	Elasticity score	36 hyper elastic cities	Elasticity score
NEWBURGH, N.Y.	4.0	Lebanon, Pa.	12.5	Alton, Ill.	21.0	Middletown, Ohio*	26.5	Gilroy, Calif.	31.5
Wilkes-Barre, Pa.*	4.0	ALBANY, N.Y.*	12.5	Pekin. Ill.	21.0	Petersburg, Va.	26.5	Norman, Okla.	32.0
Evanston, Ill.	4.0	Dover, N.J.	13.0	Neenah, Wisc.	21.0	Petaluma, Calif.	26.5	Suffolk, Va.	32.0
Miami Beach. Fla.	5.0	Port Huron, Mich.	13.0	SARASOTA, Fla.	21.0	Leavenworth, Kans.	26.5	JOHNSON CITY, Tenn.	32.0
Woonsocket, R.I.	6.0	Holyoke, Mass.*	13.0	Holland, Mich.	21.0	Boca Raton, Fla.	26.5	Chapel Hill, N.C.	32.5
ATLANTIC CITY, N.J.*	6.0	HAMILTON, Ohio*	13.0	Watsonville, Calif.	21.5	Lompoc, Calif.	27.0	Shawnee, Okla.	32.5
Camden, N.J.	7.0	Norwich, Conn.	13.0	North Chicago, Ill.	21.5	Winter Haven, Fla.	27.0	MELBOURNE, Fla.	32.5
LAWRENCE, Mass.*	7.0	Middletown, Conn.	13.0	KALAMAZOO, Mich.*	21.5	San Marcos, Tex.	27.0	Palm Springs, Calif.	32.5
Lynn, Mass.	7.0	Rome, N.Y.*	13.0	LORAIN, Ohio*	22.0	Baytown, Tex.	27.0	Longmont, Colo.	33.0
Pawtucket, R.I.	7.0	Oak Ridge, Tenn.	13.0	Massillon, Ohio	22.0	Madera, Calif.	27.5	West Memphis, Ark.	33.0
NEW LONDON, Conn.*	7.0	Rochester, N.H.	13.5	Granite City, Ill.	22.0	Palo Alto, Calif.	27.5	High Point, N.C.*	33.5
Auburn, N.Y.	7.0	Bethlehem, Pa.*	14.5	Bowling Green, Ohio	22.0	Napa, Calif.	28.0	Bristol, Tenn.	33.5
BINGHAMTON, N.Y.*	8.0	LANCASTER, Pa.*	14.5	Bradenton, Fla.	22.0	Slidell, La.	28.0	WEST PALM BEACH, Fla.	33.5
Dearborn, Mich.	8.0	CANTON, Ohio*	15.0	Clearfield, Utah	22.0	Texas City, Tex.	28.0	Port Arthur, Tex.	34.0
TRENTON, N.J.*	8.5	Alameda, Calif.	15.5	NAPLES, Fla.	22.0	Jacksonville, Ark.	28.0	LAKELAND, Fla.	34.0
Bayonne, N.J.	8.5	Meriden, Conn.	16.0	Spartanburg, S.C.	22.5	Nampa, Idaho	28.5	Springdale, Ark.	34.0
POUGHKEEPSIE, N.Y.	8.5	Attleboro, Mass.	16.0	GREENVILLE, S.C.*	22.5	Council Bluffs, Iowa	28.5	DAYTONA BEACH, Fla.	34.5
NEW BEDFORD, Mass.*	9.0	Saratoga Springs, N.Y.	16.0	Lodi, Calif.	22.5	BILOXI, Miss.	29.0	FORT MYERS, Fla.	34.5
Fall River, Mass.*	9.0	Westfield, Mass.	16.0			Waukesha, Wisc.	29.0	Bossier City, La.	34.5
		Carlisle, Pa.	16.5						

City	Value
UTICA, N.Y.*	9.5
READING, Pa.*	10.0
WILMINGTON, Del.*	10.0
Schenectady, N.Y.*	10.0
SCRANTON, Pa.*	10.0
White Plains, N.Y.	10.0
YOUNGSTOWN, Ohio*	10.5
BROCKTON, Mass.*	10.5
Troy, N.Y.*	11.0
Niagara Falls, N.Y.*	11.0
HUNTINGTON, W.V.*	11.0
East St. Louis, Ill.	11.0
Waltham, Mass.	11.0
Gloucester, Mass.	11.0
Pontiac, Mich.	11.0
Norwalk, Conn.*	11.0
YORK, Pa.*	11.5
HARRISBURG, Pa.*	11.5
SAGINAW, Mich.*	12.0
Bay City, Mich.*	12.0
East Chicago, Ind.	12.0
ANDERSON, S.C.	12.0
Ashland, Ky.*	17.0
Annapolis, Md.	17.0
Rock Island, Ill.*	17.5
SANTA BARBARA, Calif.	17.5
Monterey, Calif.	17.5
Northampton, Mass.	18.0
Warren, Ohio	18.0
MUSKEGON, Mich.	18.0
Moline, Ill.*	18.0
Springfield, Ohio*	18.5
East Lansing, Mich.	19.0
Warwick, R.I.	19.5
Gloucester, Mass.	19.5
Kannapolis, N.C.	19.5
New Albany, Ind.	20.0
SANTA CRUZ, Calif.*	20.0
Kent, Ohio	20.0
Coronado, Calif.	20.5
FORT PIERCE, Fla.	22.5
Fredericksburg, Va.	23.0
Bristol, Va.	23.0
Lancaster, Ohio	23.0
Newark, Ohio	23.5
APPLETON, Wisc.	24.0
Henderson, Ky.	24.0
Belleville, Ill.	24.0
PENSACOLA, Fla.	24.5
Elyria, Ohio*	24.5
BURLINGTON, N.C.	24.5
Elgin, Ill.	25.0
Midland, Mich.	25.0
DeKalb, Ill.	25.5
Oshkosh, Wisc.	25.5
Woodland, Calif.	25.5
CHARLESTON, W.V.*	26.0
Fairborn, Ohio	26.0
Pascagoula, Miss.	26.0
Frederick, Md.	29.0
Davis, Calif.	29.0
GALVESTON, Tex.*	29.5
Anderson, Ind.	29.5
Battle Creek, Mich.	29.5
Everett, Wash.	29.5
BOULDER, Colo.	29.5
Porterville, Calif.	29.5
Turlock, Calif.	29.5
Rock Hill, S.C.	29.5
MACON, Ga.*	30.0
Tulare, Calif.	30.0
North Little Rock, Ark.*	30.0
DAVENPORT, Iowa*	30.0
Morganton, N.C.	30.5
Santa Maria, Calif.	30.5
HICKORY, N.C.	30.5
Aiken, S.C.	30.5
CHARLESTON, S.C.*	30.5
St. Charles, Mo.	31.0
Lenoir, N.C.	31.0
Concord, N.C.	35.0
Temple, Tex.	35.0
Gastonia, N.C.	35.0
Murfreesboro, Tenn.	35.0
VISALIA, Calif.	35.5
Conway, Ark.	35.5
Kingsport, Tenn.	35.5
Gulfport, Miss.	36.0
Titusvillem Fla.	36.0
Denton, Tex.	36.0
OCALA, Fla.	36.5
FAYETTEVILLE, Ark.	36.5
Conroe, Tex.	36.5
KILEEN, Tex.	36.5
Hemet, Calif.	36.5
Fairfield, Calif.	37.0
Olathe, Kans.	37.5
	39.0
	39.0

Notes: A city in uppercase letters is considered to be the primary or historic central city for that metro area. A city in lowercase letters is considered to be a secondary city. Asterisk (*) indicates that city was designated as central city in 1950; central cities under 100,000 not evaluated because of lack of 1950 data (sometimes, not yet incorporated) are Newark, Del.; New Braunfels, Tex.; North Charleston, S.C.; Rogers, Ark.; Palm Desert and Temecula, Calif.; and Palm Bay and Port Saint Lucie, Fla.

Table A-3
149 Central Cities under 100,000 Population Primarily in Small Metro Areas (Less than 250,000)

29 zero elastic cities	Elasticity score	28 low elastic cities	Elasticity score	30 medium elastic cities	Elasticity score	29 high Elastic cities	Elasticity score	33 hyper elastic cities	Elasticity score
ALTOONA, Pa.*	4.0	SHEBOYGAN, Wisc.	14.5	OWENSBORO, KY	20.5	MANSFIELD, Ohio	26.0	DANVILLE, Va.	30.5
JOHNSTOWN, Pa.*	7.0	Marietta, Ohio	15.0	KENOSHA, Wisc.	20.5	BREMERTON, Wash.	26.0	ROCHESTER, Minn.	30.5
SHARON, Pa.	7.0	FITCHBURG, Mass.*	15.0	LAFAYETTE, Ind.	20.5	ASHEVILLE, N.C.*	26.0	DOVER, Del.	30.5
ELMIRA, N.Y.	7.0	PORTSMOUTH, N.H.	15.0	Moorhead, Minn.	20.5	FORT SMITH, Ark.	26.0	CHICO, Calif.	30.5
JAMESTOWN, N.Y.	7.0	CHARLOTTESVILLE, Va.	15.5	MONROE, La.	20.5	SAN ANGELO, Tex.*	26.0	GRAND JUNCTION, Colo.	31.0
PORTLAND, Maine*	8.0	DULUTH, Minn.*	15.5	EAU CLAIRE, Wisc.	21.0	DECATUR, Ill.*	26.5	Cedar Falls, Iowa	31.0
NEW BEDFORD, Mass.*	9.0	Urbana, Ill.	16.0	DUBUQUE, Iowa	21.5	IOWA CITY, Iowa	26.5	SHERMAN, Tex.	31.0
GLENS FALLS, N.Y.	9.0	LA CROSSE, Wisc.	16.0	YAKIMA, Wash.	21.5	LAKE CHARLES, La.	26.5	RAPID CITY, S.D.	31.0
WILLIAMSPORT, Pa.	9.0	Superior, Wisc.	16.0	FLORENCE, S.C.	21.5	BISMARCK, N.D.	26.5	El Paso de Robles, Calif.	31.0
JACKSON, Mich.*	9.0	VINELAND, N.J.	16.0	Goshen, Ind.	22.0	DAVIS, Calif.	27.0	BRYAN, Tex.	31.0
BURLINGTON, Vt.*	9.0	PARKERSBURG, W. Va.	16.5	CHEYENNE, Wyo.	22.0	LAWRENCE, Kans.	27.0	TUSCALOOSA, Ala.	31.5
BENTON HARBOR, Mich.	10.0	BELLINGHAM, Wash.	17.0	JOPLIN, Mo.	22.0	GREENVILLE, N.C.	27.0	TYLER, Tex.	31.5
WHEELING, W. Va.*	11.0	Ashland, Ore.	17.0	SANTA FE, N.M.	22.5	POCATELLO, Idaho	27.5	Texarkana, Ark.	31.5
STATE COLLEGE, Pa.	11.0	KOKOMO, Ind.	17.5	TERRE HAUTE, Ind.*	22.5	ST CLOUD, Minn.	27.5	LONGVIEW, Tex.	31.5
HAGERSTOWN, Md.	12.0	WAUSAU, Wisc.	17.5	YUBA CITY, Calif.	22.5	BILLINGS, Mont.	28.0	JACKSON, Tenn.	32.0
Bridgeton, N.J.	12.0	BANGOR, Maine	17.5	BLOOMINGTON, Ill.	23.0	GOLDSBORO, N.C.	28.0	DANBURY, Conn.*	32.0

City	Index	City	Index
PITTSFIELD, Mass.*	12.0	FLORENCE, Ala.	23.0
Weirton, W. Va.	12.0	Denison, Tex.	23.0
LEWISTON, Maine	12.0	MEDFORD, Ore.	23.0
NASHUA, N.H.*	12.0	BLOOMINGTON, Ind.	23.5
LIMA, Ohio*	12.5	OLYMPIA, Wash.	23.5
STEUBENVILLE, Ohio*	12.5	Normal, Ill.	23.5
RACINE, Wisc.*	13.0	JANESVILLE, Wisc.	23.5
CUMBERLAND, Md.	13.0	GRAND FORKS, N.D.	24.5
Leominster, Mass.	13.0	CASPER, Wyo.	24.5
Auburn, Maine	13.0	WATERLOO, Iowa*	25.0
Millville, N.J.	13.0	ALEXANDRIA, La.	25.5
BARNSTABLE, Mass.	13.0	ST JOSEPH, Mo.*	25.5
Yarmouth, Mass.	13.0	HOUMA, La.	25.5
		MERCED, Calif.	25.5

City	Index	City	Index
KANKAKEE, Ill.	18.0	SUMTER, S.C.	28.5
MUNCIE, Ind.*	18.5	VICTORIA, Tex.	28.5
GADSDEN, Ala.*	18.5	WILMINGTON, N.C.	29.0
PANAMA CITY, Fla.	18.5	LYNCHBURG, Va.	29.0
SIOUX CITY, Iowa*	18.5	RICHLAND, Wash.	29.0
CHAMPAIGN, Ill.	19.0	FARGO, N.D.	29.5
GREAT FALLS, Mont.	19.0	GREELEY, Colo.	29.5
FORT WALTON BEACH, Fla.	19.0	Hopkinsville, Ky.	29.5
Beloit, Wisc.	20.0	DOTHAN, Ala.	29.5
ELKHART, Ind.	20.0	ODESSA, Tex.	30.0
ROANOKE, Va.*	20.0	PINE BLUFF, Ark.	30.0
TEXARKANA, Tex.	20.0	Kennewick, Wash.	30.0
		Pasco, Wash.	30.0

City	Index
DECATUR, Ala.	32.5
GAINESVILLE, Fla.	33.0
ANNISTON, Ala.	33.0
HATTIESBURG, Miss.	33.0
ALBANY, Ga.	33.5
ENID, Okla.	34.0
COLUMBIA, Mo.	34.0
LAWTON, Okla.	34.0
Midland, Tex.	34.0
AUBURN, Ala.*	34.5
FLAGSTAFF, Ariz.	35.0
College Station, Tex.	36.5
LAS CRUCES, N.M.	37.5
REDDING, Calif.	37.5
Opelika, Ala.	37.5
JACKSONVILLE, N.C.	39.0
YUMA, Ariz.	39.0

Notes: A city in uppercase letters is considered to be the primary or historic central city for that metro area. A city in lowercase letters is considered to be a secondary city. Asterisk (*) indicates that city was designated as central city in 1950; central cities under 100,000 not evaluated because of lack of 1950 data (sometimes, not yet incorporated) are Corvallis, Ore.; Jonesboro, Ark.; Missoula, Mont.; Myrtle Beach, S.C.; Punta Gorda, Fla.; Rocky Mount, N.C.; and Atascadero, Paradise, and San Luis Obispo, Calif.

TABLE A-4
THREE SPECIAL CATEGORIES

Zero elasticity cities	Elasticity score	Low elasticity cities	Elasticity score	Medium elasticity cities	Elasticity score	High elasticity cities	Elasticity score	Hyper elasticity cities	Elasticity score
				8 Mexican Border Towns in 4 Metro Areas					
				Harlingen, Tex.	20.5	MCALLEN, Tex.	27.0	BROWNSVILLE, Tex.	32.0
				San Benito, Tex.	23.0	Mission, Tex.	30.0	EL PASO, Tex.*	33.0
						LAREDO, Tex.	30.5	Edinburg, Tex.	35.5
				11 White America Cities in 7 Metro Areas					
		SPOKANE, Wash.*	17.0	PROVO, Utah	23.5	EUGENE, Ore.	26.5		
				Orem, Utah	23.5	Springfield, Ore.	26.5		
				SALT LAKE CITY, Utah*	24.0	SPRINGFIELD, Mo.*	28.0		
				Ogden, Utah*	24.0	BOISE CITY, Idaho	28.5		
						FORT COLLINS, Colo.	30.0		
						Loveland, Colo.	30.0		

6 Central City-less Metro Areas

BERGEN-PASSAIC, N.J.
BRAZORIA, Tex.
HONOLULU, Hawaii
MIDDLESEX-SOMERSET-
    HUNTERDON, N.J.
MONMOUTH-OCEAN, N.J.
NASSAU-SUFFOLK, N.Y.

Notes: A city in uppercase letters is considered to be the primary or historic central city for that metro area. A city in lowercase letters is considered to be a secondary city. Asterisk (*) indicates that city was designated as central city in 1950; approximately 30 other cities from Tables A-2 and A-3 would qualify as White America cities

Sources

All data not otherwise indicated are taken from either publications or the website of the Bureau of the Census of the U.S. Department of Commerce (<http://www.census.gov>). These cover the decennial censuses from 1950 to 2000 as well as the annual *Statistical Abstract of the United States* and the *Census of Governments.*

Metropolitan racial segregation indices for both housing markets and elementary schools are provided by the website of the Lewis Mumford Center for Comparative Urban and Regional Research of the State University of New York at Albany (<http://mumford1.dyndns.org/cen2000/WholePop/WPseg-data.htm>).

Economic segregation indices for 1970 are found in Alan J. Abramson, Mitchell S. Tobin, and Matthew R. VanderGoot, "The Changing Geography of Metropolitan Opportunity: The Segregation of the Poor in U.S. Metropolitan Areas, 1970 to 1990," in Fannie Mae: *Housing Policy Debate* 6, no. 1, 45–72. For 1980 to 2000 these calculations have been updated by Peter A. Tatian and Alisa Wilson (forthcoming), *Segregation of the Poor in U.S. Metropolitan Areas,* Neighborhood Change in Urban America Research Series, Washington, D.C.: The Urban Institute. There are small differences in the delineation of some metropolitan areas between 1970 and later decades.

All information on metro area employment and personal income trends comes from the Regional Economic Information Service of the Bureau of Economic Analysis of the U.S. Department of Commerce (<http://www.bea.doc.gov/bea/regional/reis>).

The source for municipal bond ratings is the October 2002 edition of Mergent Bond Record (<http://www.mergent.com>) for ratings provided by Moody's Investors Service.

The analysis of state laws regarding city-county consolidation, municipal formation, and annexation powers is adapted from

State Laws Governing Local Government and Administration published by the U.S. Advisory Commission on Intergovernmental
Relations (March 1993). Table 1.6 is adapted from an earlier
study of the same title by Melvin. B. Hill, Jr., et al., the Institute
of Government, University of Georgia (1971).

Finally, readers with questions or seeking information may
contact me by phone: (202) 364-2455; fax (202) 364-6936;
email (drusk@starpower.net) or visit my website (<http://www.
DavidRusk.com>).

Index

Note: The notations n and *t* after page numbers refer to notes and tables respectively.

About the Center

The Center is the living memorial of the United States of America to the nation's twenty-eighth president, Woodrow Wilson. Congress established the Woodrow Wilson Center in 1968 as an international institute for advanced study, "symbolizing and strengthening the fruitful relationship between the world of learning and the world of public affairs." The Center opened in 1970 under its own board of trustees.

In all its activities the Woodrow Wilson Center is a nonprofit, nonpartisan organization, supported financially by annual appropriations from the Congress, and by the contributions of foundations, corporations, and individuals. Conclusions or opinions expressed in Center publications and programs are those of the authors and speakers and do not necessarily reflect the views of the Center staff, fellows, trustees, advisory groups, or any individuals or organizations that provide financial support to the Center.